INTELLIGENCE AND COUNTERINTELLIGENCE STUDIES

BALANCING LIBERTY, PRIVACY, AND SECURITY WITH INTELLIGENCE CAPABILITIES

ANALYSES AND RECOMMENDATIONS

INTELLIGENCE AND COUNTERINTELLIGENCE STUDIES

Additional books in this series can be found on Nova's website under the Series tab.

Additional e-books in this series can be found on Nova's website under the e-book tab.

INTELLIGENCE AND COUNTERINTELLIGENCE STUDIES

BALANCING LIBERTY, PRIVACY, AND SECURITY WITH INTELLIGENCE CAPABILITIES

ANALYSES AND RECOMMENDATIONS

BENJI NORWOOD
EDITOR

nova publishers
New York

For permission to use material from this book please contact us:
Telephone 631-231-7269; Fax 631-231-8175
Web Site: http://www.novapublishers.com

Library of Congress Cataloging-in-Publication Data

ISBN: 978-1-63117-999-0

Published by Nova Science Publishers, Inc. † New York

CONTENTS

PREFACE

This book presents the final report of the review group on intelligence and communications technologies. Recommendations are provided that are designed to protect national security and maintain intelligence capabilities while also respecting our longstanding commitment to privacy, civil liberties, and the trust of allies abroad, with due consideration of reducing the risk of unauthorized disclosures.

Chapter 1 – On August 27, 2013, the President announced the creation of the Review Group on Intelligence and Communications Technologies. The immediate backdrop for their work was a series of disclosures of classified information involving foreign intelligence collection by the National Security Agency. The disclosures revealed intercepted collections that occurred inside and outside of the United States and that included the communications of United States persons and legal permanent residents, as well as non-United States persons located outside the United States. Although these disclosures and the responses and concerns of many people in the United States and abroad have informed this Report, the authors have focused more broadly on the creation of sturdy foundations for the future, safeguarding liberty and security in a rapidly changing world.

Chapter 2 – In the latter half of 2013 and early 2014, the United States Government undertook a broad-ranging and unprecedented review of their signals intelligence programs, led by the White House with relevant Departments and Agencies across the Government. In addition to their own intensive work, the review process drew on input from key stakeholders, including Congress, the tech community, civil society, foreign partners, the Review Group on Intelligence and Communication Technologies, the Privacy and Civil Liberties Oversight Board, and others. The Administration's review examined how, in light of new and changing technologies, the authors can use their intelligence capabilities in a way that optimally protects their national security while supporting their foreign policy, respecting privacy and civil liberties, maintaining the public trust, and reducing the risk of unauthorized disclosures. On January 17, 2014, the President delivered a speech at the Department of Justice to announce the outcomes of this review process.

In that speech, the President made clear that the men and women of the U.S. intelligence community, including the NSA, consistently follow those protocols designed to protect the privacy of ordinary people and are not abusing authorities. When mistakes have been made, they have corrected those mistakes. But for their intelligence community to be effective over the long haul, the authors must maintain the trust of the American people, and people around the world. To that end, the Administration has developed a path forward that the authors believe should give the American people greater confidence that their rights are being protected, while preserving important tools that keep us safe, and that addresses significant questions that have been raised overseas. Today the President announced the Administration's adoption of a series of concrete and substantial reforms that the Administration will adopt administratively or seek to codify with Congress, to include a majority of the recommendations.

Chapter 3 – The United States, like other nations, has gathered intelligence throughout its history to ensure that national security and foreign policy decisionmakers have access to timely, accurate, and insightful information.

The collection of signals intelligence is necessary for the United States to advance its national security and foreign policy interests and to protect its citizens and the citizens of its allies and partners from harm. At the same time, signals intelligence activities and the possibility that such activities may be improperly disclosed to the public pose multiple risks. These include risks to: their relationships with other nations, including the cooperation the authors receive from other nations on law enforcement, counterterrorism, and other issues; their commercial, economic, and financial interests, including a potential loss of international trust in U.S. firms and the decreased willingness of other nations to participate in international data sharing, privacy, and regulatory regimes; the credibility of their commitment to an open, interoperable, and secure global Internet; and the protection of intelligence sources and methods.

In addition, their signals intelligence activities must take into account that all persons should be treated with dignity and respect, regardless of their nationality or wherever they might reside, and that all persons have legitimate privacy interests in the handling of their personal information.

Chapter 4 – On January 17, 2014, President Obama gave a speech at the Department of Justice on his Administration's review of certain intelligence activities. During this speech, he ordered a transition that would end the Section 215 bulk telephony metadata program as it previously existed and establish a new mechanism to preserve the capabilities the authors need without the government holding this bulk metadata. The President made clear that he was ordering this transition to give the public greater confidence that their privacy is appropriately protected, while maintaining the tools their intelligence and law enforcement agencies need to keep us safe. This fact sheet describes the steps the Administration has taken to implement this transition, details the President's proposal for a new program to replace the Section 215 program, and outlines the steps the Administration will be taking in the near future to realize the President's vision.

In: Balancing Liberty, Privacy, and Security …
Editor: Benji Norwood

ISBN: 978-1-63117-999-0

Chapter 1

LIBERTY AND SECURITY IN A CHANGING WORLD*

President's Review Group on Intelligence and Communications Technologies

ACKNOWLEDGMENTS

The Review Group would like to thank the many people who supported our efforts in preparing this Report. A number of people were formally assigned to assist the Group, and all performed with professionalism, hard work, and good cheer. These included Brett Freedman, Kenneth Gould, and other personnel from throughout the government. We thank as well the many other people both inside and outside of the government who have contributed their time and energy to assisting in our work.

INTRODUCTION

On August 27, 2013, the President announced the creation of the Review Group on Intelligence and Communications Technologies. The immediate backdrop for our work was a series of disclosures of classified information involving foreign intelligence collection by the National Security Agency. The disclosures revealed intercepted collections that occurred inside and outside of the United States and that included the communications of United States persons and legal permanent residents, as well as non-United States persons located outside the United States. Although these disclosures and the responses and concerns of many people in the United States and abroad have informed this Report, we have focused more broadly on the creation of sturdy foundations for the future, safeguarding (as our title suggests) liberty and security in a rapidly changing world.

Those rapid changes include unprecedented advances in information and communications technologies; increased globalization of trade, investment, and information flows; and fluid national security threats against which the American public rightly expects its government to

* This is an edited, reformatted and augmented version of a Final Report, dated December 12, 2013.

provide protection. With this larger context in mind, we have been mindful of significant recent changes in the environment in which intelligence collection takes place.

For example, traditional distinctions between "foreign" and "domestic" are far less clear today than in the past, now that the same communications devices, software, and networks are used globally by friends and foes alike. These changes, as well as changes in the nature of the threats we face, have implications for the right of privacy, our strategic relationships with other nations, and the levels of innovation and information-sharing that underpin key elements of the global economy.

In addressing these issues, the United States must pursue multiple and often competing goals at home and abroad. In facing these challenges, the United States must take into account the full range of interests and values that it is pursuing, and it must communicate these goals to the American public and to key international audiences. These goals include:

Protecting The Nation Against Threats to Our National Security. The ability of the United States to combat threats from state rivals, terrorists, and weapons proliferators depends on the acquisition of foreign intelligence information from a broad range of sources and through a variety of methods. In an era increasingly dominated by technological advances in communications technologies, the United States must continue to collect signals intelligence globally in order to assure the safety of our citizens at home and abroad and to help protect the safety of our friends, our allies, and the many nations with whom we have cooperative relationships.

Promoting Other National Security and Foreign Policy Interests. Intelligence is designed not only to protect against threats but also to safeguard a wide range of national security and foreign policy interests, including counterintelligence, counteracting the international elements of organized crime, and preventing drug trafficking, human trafficking, and mass atrocities.

Protecting the Right to Privacy. The right to privacy is essential to a free and self-governing society. The rise of modern technologies makes it all the more important that democratic nations respect people's fundamental right to privacy, which is a defining part of individual security and personal liberty.

Protecting Democracy, Civil Liberties, and the Rule of Law. Free debate within the United States is essential to the long-term vitality of American democracy and helps bolster democracy globally. Excessive surveillance and unjustified secrecy can threaten civil liberties, public trust, and the core processes of democratic self-government. All parts of the government, including those that protect our national security, must be subject to the rule of law.

Promoting Prosperity, Security, and Openness in a Networked World. The United States must adopt and sustain policies that support technological innovation and collaboration both at home and abroad. Such policies are central to economic growth, which is promoted in turn by economic freedom and spurring entrepreneurship. For this reason, the United States must continue to establish and strengthen international norms of Internet freedom and security.

Protecting Strategic Alliances. The collection of intelligence must be undertaken in a way that preserves and strengthens our strategic relationships. We must be respectful of those relationships and of the leaders and citizens of other nations, especially those with whom we share interests, values, or both. The collection of intelligence should be undertaken in a way that recognizes the importance of cooperative relationships with other nations and that respects the legitimate privacy interests and the dignity of those outside our borders.

The challenge of managing these often competing goals is daunting. But it is a challenge that the nation must meet if it is to live up to its promises to its citizens and to posterity.

EXECUTIVE SUMMARY

Overview

The national security threats facing the United States and our allies are numerous and significant, and they will remain so well into the future. These threats include international terrorism, the proliferation of weapons of mass destruction, and cyber espionage and warfare. A robust foreign intelligence collection capability is essential if we are to protect ourselves against such threats. Because our adversaries operate through the use of complex communications technologies, the National Security Agency, with its impressive capabilities and talented officers, is indispensable to keeping our country and our allies safe and secure.

At the same time, the United States is deeply committed to the protection of privacy and civil liberties—fundamental values that can be and at times have been eroded by excessive intelligence collection. After careful consideration, we recommend a number of changes to our intelligence collection activities that will protect these values without undermining what we need to do to keep our nation safe.

Principles

We suggest careful consideration of the following principles:

1. ***The United States Government must protect, at once, two different forms of security: national security and personal privacy.***
   In the American tradition, the word "security" has had multiple meanings. In contemporary parlance, it often refers to *national security* or *homeland security*. One of the government's most fundamental responsibilities is to protect this form of security, broadly understood. At the same time, the idea of security refers to a quite different and equally fundamental value, captured in the Fourth Amendment to the United States Constitution: "The right of the people to be *secure* in their persons, houses, papers, and effects, against unreasonable searches and seizures, shall not be violated ... " (emphasis added). Both forms of security must be protected.
2. ***The central task is one of risk management; multiple risks are involved, and all of them must be considered.***

When public officials acquire foreign intelligence information, they seek to reduce risks, above all risks to national security. The challenge, of course, is that multiple risks are involved. Government must consider all of those risks, not a subset, when it is creating sensible safeguards. In addition to reducing risks to national security, public officials must consider four other risks:

- Risks to privacy;
- Risks to freedom and civil liberties, on the Internet and elsewhere;
- Risks to our relationships with other nations; and
- Risks to trade and commerce, including international commerce.

3. ***The idea of "balancing" has an important element of truth, but it is also inadequate and misleading.***
   It is tempting to suggest that the underlying goal is to achieve the right "balance" between the two forms of security. The suggestion has an important element of truth. But some safeguards are not subject to balancing at all. In a free society, public officials should never engage in surveillance in order to punish their political enemies; to restrict freedom of speech or religion; to suppress legitimate criticism and dissent; to help their preferred companies or industries; to provide domestic companies with an unfair competitive advantage; or to benefit or burden members of groups defined in terms of religion, ethnicity, race, and gender.
4. ***The government should base its decisions on a careful analysis of consequences, including both benefits and costs (to the extent feasible).***
   In many areas of public policy, officials are increasingly insistent on the need for careful analysis of the consequences of their decisions, and on the importance of relying not on intuitions and anecdotes, but on evidence and data. Before they are undertaken, surveillance decisions should depend (to the extent feasible) on a careful assessment of the anticipated consequences, including the full range of relevant risks. Such decisions should also be subject to continuing scrutiny, including retrospective analysis, to ensure that any errors are corrected.

Surveillance of US Persons

With respect to surveillance of US Persons, we recommend a series of significant reforms. Under section 215 of the Foreign Intelligence Surveillance Act (FISA), the government now stores bulk telephony meta-data, understood as information that includes the telephone numbers that both originate and receive calls, time of call, and date of call. (Meta-data does not include the content of calls.). We recommend that Congress should end such storage and transition to a system in which such meta- data is held privately for the government to query when necessary for national security purposes.

In our view, the current storage by the government of bulk meta-data creates potential risks to public trust, personal privacy, and civil liberty. We recognize that the government might need access to such meta-data, which should be held instead either by private providers or by a private third party. This approach would allow the government access to the relevant information when such access is justified, and thus protect national security without unnecessarily threatening privacy and liberty. Consistent with this recommendation, we endorse a broad principle for the future: as a general rule and without senior policy review, the government should not be permitted to collect and store mass, undigested, non-public personal information about US persons for the purpose of enabling future queries and data-mining for foreign intelligence purposes.

We also recommend specific reforms that will provide Americans with greater safeguards against intrusions into their personal domain. We endorse new steps to protect American citizens engaged in communications with non-US persons. We recommend important restrictions on the ability of the Foreign Intelligence Surveillance Court (FISC) to compel third parties (such as telephone service providers) to disclose private information to the government. We endorse similar restrictions on the issuance of National Security Letters (by which the Federal Bureau of Investigation now compels individuals and organizations to turn over certain otherwise private records), recommending prior judicial review except in emergencies, where time is of the essence.

We recommend concrete steps to promote transparency and accountability, and thus to promote public trust, which is essential in this domain. Legislation should be enacted requiring information about surveillance programs to be made available to the Congress and to the American people to the greatest extent possible (subject only to the need to protect classified information). We also recommend that legislation should be enacted authorizing telephone, Internet, and other providers to disclose publicly general information about orders they receive directing them to provide information to the government. Such information might disclose the number of orders that providers have received, the broad categories of information produced, and the number of users whose information has been produced. In the same vein, we recommend that the government should publicly disclose, on a regular basis, general data about the orders it has issued in programs whose existence is unclassified.

Surveillance of Non-US Persons

Significant steps should be taken to protect the privacy of non-US persons. In particular, any programs that allow surveillance of such persons even outside the United States should satisfy six separate constraints. They:

1) must be authorized by duly enacted laws or properly authorized executive orders;
2) must be directed *exclusively* at protecting national security interests of the United States or our allies;
3) must *not* be directed at illicit or illegitimate ends, such as the theft of trade secrets or obtaining commercial gain for domestic industries;
4) must not target any non-United States person based solely on that person's political views or religious convictions;
5) must not disseminate information about non-United States persons if the information is not relevant to protecting the national security of the United States or our allies; and
6) must be subject to careful oversight and to the highest degree of transparency consistent with protecting the national security of the United States and our allies.

We recommend that, in the absence of a specific and compelling showing, the US Government should follow the model of the Department of Homeland Security and apply the Privacy Act of 1974 in the same way to both US persons and non-US persons.

Setting Priorities and Avoiding Unjustified or Unnecessary Surveillance

To reduce the risk of unjustified, unnecessary, or excessive surveillance in foreign nations, including collection on foreign leaders, we recommend that the President should create a new process, requiring highest-level approval of all sensitive intelligence requirements and the methods that the Intelligence Community will use to meet them. This process should identify both the uses and the limits of surveillance on foreign leaders and in foreign nations.

We recommend that those involved in the process should consider whether (1) surveillance is motivated by especially important national security concerns or by concerns that are less pressing and (2) surveillance would involve leaders of nations with whom we share fundamental values and interests or leaders of other nations. With close reference to (2), we recommend that with a small number of closely allied governments, meeting specific criteria, the US Government should explore understandings or arrangements regarding intelligence collection guidelines and practices with respect to each others' citizens (including, if and where appropriate, intentions, strictures, or limitations with respect to collections).

Organizational Reform

We recommend a series of organizational changes. With respect to the National Security Agency (NSA), we believe that the Director should be a Senate-confirmed position, with civilians eligible to hold that position; the President should give serious consideration to making the next Director of NSA a civilian. NSA should be clearly designated as a foreign intelligence organization. Other missions (including that of NSA's Information Assurance Directorate) should generally be assigned elsewhere. The head of the military unit, US Cyber Command, and the Director of NSA should not be a single official.

We favor a newly chartered, strengthened, independent Civil Liberties and Privacy Protection Board (CLPP Board) to replace the Privacy and Civil Liberties Oversight Board (PCLOB). The CLPP Board should have broad authority to review government activity relating to foreign intelligence and counterterrorism whenever that activity has implications for civil liberties and privacy. A Special Assistant to the President for Privacy should also be designated, serving in both the Office of Management and Budget and the National Security Staff. This Special Assistant should chair a Chief Privacy Officer Council to help coordinate privacy policy throughout the Executive branch.

With respect to the FISC, we recommend that Congress should create the position of Public Interest Advocate to represent the interests of privacy and civil liberties before the FISC. We also recommend that the government should take steps to increase the transparency of the FISC's decisions and that Congress should change the process by which judges are appointed to the FISC.

Global Communications Technology

Substantial steps should be taken to protect prosperity, security, and openness in a networked world. A free and open Internet is critical to both self-government and economic growth.

The United States Government should reaffirm the 2011 International Strategy for Cyberspace. It should stress that Internet governance must not be limited to governments, but should include all appropriate stakeholders, including businesses, civil society, and technology specialists.

The US Government should take additional steps to promote security, by (1) fully supporting and not undermining efforts to create encryption standards; (2) making clear that it will not in any way subvert, undermine, weaken, or make vulnerable generally available commercial encryption; and (3) supporting efforts to encourage the greater use of encryption technology for data in transit, at rest, in the cloud, and in storage. Among other measures relevant to the Internet, the US Government should also support international norms or agreements to increase confidence in the security of online communications.

For big data and data-mining programs directed at communications, the US Government should develop Privacy and Civil Liberties Impact Assessments to ensure that such efforts are statistically reliable, cost- effective, and protective of privacy and civil liberties.

Protecting What We Do Collect

We recommend a series of steps to reduce the risks associated with "insider threats." A governing principle is plain: Classified information should be shared only with those who genuinely need to know. We recommend specific changes to improve the efficacy of the personnel vetting system. The use of "for-profit" corporations to conduct personnel investigations should be reduced or terminated. Security clearance levels should be further differentiated. Departments and agencies should institute a Work-Related Access approach to the dissemination of sensitive, classified information. Employees with high-level security clearances should be subject to a Personnel Continuous Monitoring Program. Ongoing security clearance vetting of individuals should use a risk- management approach and depend on the sensitivity and quantity of the programs and information to which individuals are given access.

The security of information technology networks carrying classified information should be a matter of ongoing concern by Principals, who should conduct an annual assessment with the assistance of a "second opinion" team. Classified networks should increase the use of physical and logical separation of data to restrict access, including through Information Rights Management software. Cyber-security software standards and practices on classified networks should be at least as good as those on the most secure private-sector enterprises.

Recommendations

Recommendation 1

We recommend that section 215 should be amended to authorize the Foreign Intelligence Surveillance Court to issue a section 215 order compelling a third party to disclose otherwise private information about particular individuals only if:

(1) it finds that the government has reasonable grounds to believe that the particular information sought is relevant to an authorized investigation intended to protect "against international terrorism or clandestine intelligence activities" and
(2) like a subpoena, the order is reasonable in focus, scope, and breadth.

Recommendation 2

We recommend that statutes that authorize the issuance of National Security Letters should be amended to permit the issuance of National Security Letters only upon a judicial finding that:

(1) the government has reasonable grounds to believe that the particular information sought is relevant to an authorized investigation intended to protect "against international terrorism or clandestine intelligence activities" and
(2) like a subpoena, the order is reasonable in focus, scope, and breadth.

Recommendation 3

We recommend that all statutes authorizing the use of National Security Letters should be amended to require the use of the same oversight, minimization, retention, and dissemination standards that currently govern the use of section 215 orders.

Recommendation 4

We recommend that, as a general rule, and without senior policy review, the government should not be permitted to collect and store all mass, undigested, non-public personal information about individuals to enable future queries and data-mining for foreign intelligence purposes. Any program involving government collection or storage of such data must be narrowly tailored to serve an important government interest.

Recommendation 5

We recommend that legislation should be enacted that terminates the storage of bulk telephony meta-data by the government under section 215, and transitions as soon as reasonably possible to a system in which such meta-data is held instead either by private providers or by a private third party. Access to such data should be permitted only with a section 215 order from the Foreign Intellience Surveillance Court that meets the requirements set forth in Recommendation 1.

Recommendation 6

We recommend that the government should commission a study of the legal and policy options for assessing the distinction between meta- data and other types of information. The study should include technological experts and persons with a diverse range of perspectives, including experts about the missions of intelligence and law enforcement agencies and about privacy and civil liberties.

Recommendation 7

We recommend that legislation should be enacted requiring that detailed information about authorities such as those involving National Security Letters, section 215 business records, section 702, pen register and trap-and-trace, and the section 215 bulk telephony meta-data program should be made available on a regular basis to Congress and the American people to the greatest extent possible, consistent with the need to protect classified information. With respect to authorities and programs whose existence is unclassified, there should be a strong presumption of transparency to enable the American people and their elected representatives independently to assess the merits of the programs for themselves.

Recommendation 8

We recommend that:

(1) legislation should be enacted providing that, in the use of National Security Letters, section 215 orders, pen register and trap-and-trace orders, 702 orders, and similar orders directing individuals, businesses, or other institutions to turn over information to the government, non-disclosure orders may be issued only upon a judicial finding that there are reasonable grounds to believe that disclosure would significantly threaten the national security, interfere with an ongoing investigation, endanger the life or physical safety of any person, impair diplomatic relations, or put at risk some other similarly weighty government or foreign intelligence interest;

(2) nondisclosure orders should remain in effect for no longer than 180 days without judicial re-approval; and

(3) nondisclosure orders should never be issued in a manner that prevents the recipient of the order from seeking legal counsel in order to challenge the order's legality.

Recommendation 9

We recommend that legislation should be enacted providing that, even when nondisclosure orders are appropriate, recipients of National Security Letters, section 215 orders, pen register and trap-and-trace orders, section 702 orders, and similar orders issued in programs whose existence is unclassified may publicly disclose on a periodic basis general information about the number of such orders they have received, the number they have complied with, the general categories of information they have produced, and the number of users whose information they have produced in each category, unless the government makes a compelling demonstration that such disclosures would endanger the national security.

Recommendation 10

We recommend that, building on current law, the government should publicly disclose on a regular basis general data about National Security Letters, section 215 orders, pen register and trap-and-trace orders, section 702 orders, and similar orders in programs whose existence is unclassified, unless the government makes a compelling demonstration that such disclosures would endanger the national security.

Recommendation 11

We recommend that the decision to keep secret from the American people programs of the magnitude of the section 215 bulk telephony meta-data program should be made only after careful deliberation at high levels of government and only with due consideration of and respect for the strong presumption of transparency that is central to democratic governance. A program of this magnitude should be kept secret from the American people only if (a) the program serves a compelling governmental interest and (b) the efficacy of the program would be *substantially* impaired if our enemies were to know of its existence.

Recommendation 12

We recommend that, if the government legally intercepts a communication under section 702, or under any other authority that justifies the interception of a communication on the ground that it is directed at a non-United States person who is located outside the United States, and if the communication either includes a United States person as a participant or reveals information about a United States person:

(1) any information about that United States person should be purged upon detection unless it either has foreign intelligence value or is necessary to prevent serious harm to others;
(2) any information about the United States person may not be used in evidence in any proceeding against that United States person;
(3) the government may not search the contents of communications acquired under section 702, or under any other authority covered by this recommendation, in an effort to identify communications of particular United States persons, except (a) when the information is necessary to prevent a threat of death or serious bodily harm, or (b) when the government obtains a warrant based on probable cause to believe that the United States person is planning or is engaged in acts of international terrorism.

Recommendation 13

We recommend that, in implementing section 702, and any other authority that authorizes the surveillance of non-United States persons who are outside the United States, in addition to the safeguards and oversight mechanisms already in place, the US Government should reaffirm that such surveillance:

(1) must be authorized by duly enacted laws or properly authorized executive orders;
(2) must be directed *exclusively* at the national security of the United States or our allies;
(3) must *not* be directed at illicit or illegitimate ends, such as the theft of trade secrets or obtaining commercial gain for domestic industries; and
(4) must not disseminate information about non-United States persons if the information is not relevant to protecting the national security of the United States or our allies.

In addition, the US Government should make clear that such surveillance:

(1) must not target any non-United States person located outside of the United States based solely on that person's political views or religious convictions; and
(2) must be subject to careful oversight and to the highest degree of transparency consistent with protecting the national security of the United States and our allies.

Recommendation 14

We recommend that, in the absence of a specific and compelling showing, the US Government should follow the model of the Department of Homeland Security, and apply the Privacy Act of 1974 in the same way to both US persons and non-US persons.

Recommendation 15

We recommend that the National Security Agency should have a limited statutory emergency authority to continue to track known targets of counterterrorism surveillance when they first enter the United States, until the Foreign Intelligence Surveillance Court has time to issue an order authorizing continuing surveillance inside the United States.

Recommendation 16

We recommend that the President should create a new process requiring high-level approval of all sensitive intelligence requirements and the methods the Intelligence Community will use to meet them. This process should, among other things, identify both the uses and limits of surveillance on foreign leaders and in foreign nations. A small staff of policy and intelligence professionals should review intelligence collection for sensitive activities on an ongoing basis throughout the year and advise the National Security Council Deputies and Principals when they believe that an unscheduled review by them may be warranted.

Recommendation 17

We recommend that:

(1) senior policymakers should review not only the requirements in Tier One and Tier Two of the National Intelligence Priorities Framework, but also any other requirements that they define as sensitive;
(2) senior policymakers should review the methods and targets of collection on requirements in any Tier that they deem sensitive; and
(3) senior policymakers from the federal agencies with responsibility for US economic interests should participate in the review process because disclosures of classified information can have detrimental effects on US economic interests.

Recommendation 18

We recommend that the Director of National Intelligence should establish a mechanism to monitor the collection and dissemination activities of the Intelligence Community to ensure they are consistent with the determinations of senior policymakers. To this end, the Director of National Intelligence should prepare an annual report on this issue to the National Security Advisor, to be shared with the Congressional intelligence committees.

Recommendation 19

We recommend that decisions to engage in surveillance of foreign leaders should consider the following criteria:

(1) Is there a need to engage in such surveillance in order to assess significant threats to our national security?
(2) Is the other nation one with whom we share values and interests, with whom we have a cooperative relationship, and whose leaders we should accord a high degree of respect and deference?
(3) Is there a reason to believe that the foreign leader may be being duplicitous in dealing with senior US officials or is attempting to hide information relevant to national security concerns from the US?
(4) Are there other collection means or collection targets that could reliably reveal the needed information?
(5) What would be the negative effects if the leader became aware of the US collection, or if citizens of the relevant nation became so aware?

Recommendation 20

We recommend that the US Government should examine the feasibility of creating software that would allow the National Security Agency and other intelligence agencies more easily to conduct targeted information acquisition rather than bulk-data collection.

Recommendation 21

We recommend that with a small number of closely allied governments, meeting specific criteria, the US Government should explore understandings or arrangements regarding intelligence collection guidelines and practices with respect to each others' citizens (including, if and where appropriate, intentions, strictures, or limitations with respect to collections). The criteria should include:

(1) shared national security objectives;
(2) a close, open, honest, and cooperative relationship between senior-level policy officials; and
(3) a relationship between intelligence services characterized both by the sharing of intelligence information and analytic thinking and by operational cooperation against critical targets of joint national security concern. Discussions of such understandings or arrangements should be done between relevant intelligence communities, with senior policy-level oversight.

Recommendation 22

We recommend that:

(1) the Director of the National Security Agency should be a Senate-confirmed position;
(2) civilians should be eligible to hold that position; and

(3) the President should give serious consideration to making the next Director of the National Security Agency a civilian.

Recommendation 23

We recommend that the National Security Agency should be clearly designated as a foreign intelligence organization; missions other than foreign intelligence collection should generally be reassigned elsewhere.

Recommendation 24

We recommend that the head of the military unit, US Cyber Command, and the Director of the National Security Agency should not be a single official.

Recommendation 25

We recommend that the Information Assurance Directorate—a large component of the National Security Agency that is not engaged in activities related to foreign intelligence—should become a separate agency within the Department of Defense, reporting to the cyber policy element within the Office of the Secretary of Defense.

Recommendation 26

We recommend the creation of a privacy and civil liberties policy official located both in the National Security Staff and the Office of Management and Budget.

Recommendation 27

We recommend that:

(1) The charter of the Privacy and Civil Liberties Oversight Board should be modified to create a new and strengthened agency, the Civil Liberties and Privacy Protection Board, that can oversee Intelligence Community activities for foreign intelligence purposes, rather than only for counterterrorism purposes;

(2) The Civil Liberties and Privacy Protection Board should be an authorized recipient for whistle-blower complaints related to privacy and civil liberties concerns from employees in the Intelligence Community;

(3) An Office of Technology Assessment should be created within the Civil Liberties and Privacy Protection Board to assess Intelligence Community technology initiatives and support privacy-enhancing technologies; and

(4) Some compliance functions, similar to outside auditor functions in corporations, should be shifted from the National Security Agency and perhaps other intelligence agencies to the Civil Liberties and Privacy Protection Board.

Recommendation 28

We recommend that:

(1) Congress should create the position of Public Interest Advocate to represent privacy and civil liberties interests before the Foreign Intelligence Surveillance Court;
(2) the Foreign Intelligence Surveillance Court should have greater technological expertise available to the judges;
(3) the transparency of the Foreign Intelligence Surveillance Court's decisions should be increased, including by instituting declassification reviews that comply with existing standards; and
(4) Congress should change the process by which judges are appointed to the Foreign Intelligence Surveillance Court, with the appointment power divided among the Supreme Court Justices.

Recommendation 29

We recommend that, regarding encryption, the US Government should:

(1) fully support and not undermine efforts to create encryption standards;
(2) not in any way subvert, undermine, weaken, or make vulnerable generally available commercial software; and
(3) increase the use of encryption and urge US companies to do so, in order to better protect data in transit, at rest, in the cloud, and in other storage.

Recommendation 30

We recommend that the National Security Council staff should manage an interagency process to review on a regular basis the activities of the US Government regarding attacks that exploit a previously unknown vulnerability in a computer application or system. These are often called "Zero Day" attacks because developers have had zero days to address and patch the vulnerability. US policy should generally move to ensure that Zero Days are quickly blocked, so that the underlying vulnerabilities are patched on US Government and other networks. In rare instances, US policy may briefly authorize using a Zero Day for high priority intelligence collection, following senior, interagency review involving all appropriate departments.

Recommendation 31

We recommend that the United States should support international norms or international agreements for specific measures that will increase confidence in the security of online communications. Among those measures to be considered are:

(1) Governments should not use surveillance to steal industry secrets to advantage their domestic industry;
(2) Governments should not use their offensive cyber capabilities to change the amounts held in financial accounts or otherwise manipulate the financial systems;
(3) Governments should promote transparency about the number and type of law enforcement and other requests made to communications providers;
(4) Absent a specific and compelling reason, governments should avoid localization requirements that (a) mandate location of servers and other information technology facilities or (b) prevent trans-border data flows.

Recommendation 32

We recommend that there be an Assistant Secretary of State to lead diplomacy of international information technology issues.

Recommendation 33

We recommend that as part of its diplomatic agenda on international information technology issues, the United States should advocate for, and explain its rationale for, a model of Internet governance that is inclusive of all appropriate stakeholders, not just governments.

Recommendation 34

We recommend that the US Government should streamline the process for lawful international requests to obtain electronic communications through the Mutual Legal Assistance Treaty process.

Recommendation 35

We recommend that for big data and data-mining programs directed at communications, the US Government should develop Privacy and Civil Liberties Impact Assessments to ensure that such efforts are statistically reliable, cost-effective, and protective of privacy and civil liberties.

Recommendation 36

We recommend that for future developments in communications technology, the US should create program-by-program reviews informed by expert technologists, to assess and respond to emerging privacy and civil liberties issues, through the Civil Liberties and Privacy Protection Board or other agencies.

Recommendation 37

We recommend that the US Government should move toward a system in which background investigations relating to the vetting of personnel for security clearance are performed solely by US Government employees or by a non-profit, private sector corporation.

Recommendation 38

We recommend that the vetting of personnel for access to classified information should be ongoing, rather than periodic. A standard of Personnel Continuous Monitoring should be adopted, incorporating data from Insider Threat programs and from commercially available sources, to note such things as changes in credit ratings or any arrests or court proceedings.

Recommendation 39

We recommend that security clearances should be more highly differentiated, including the creation of "administrative access" clearances that allow for support and information technology personnel to have the access they need without granting them unnecessary access to substantive policy or intelligence material.

Recommendation 40

We recommend that the US Government should institute a demonstration project in which personnel with security clearances would be given an Access Score, based upon the sensitivity of the information to which they have access and the number and sensitivity of Special Access Programs and Compartmented Material clearances they have. Such an Access Score should be periodically updated.

Recommendation 41

We recommend that the "need-to-share" or "need-to-know" models should be replaced with a Work-Related Access model, which would ensure that all personnel whose role requires access to specific information have such access, without making the data more generally available to cleared personnel who are merely interested.

Recommendation 42

We recommend that the Government networks carrying Secret and higher classification information should use the best available cyber security hardware, software, and procedural protections against both external and internal threats. The National Security Advisor and the Director of the Office of Management and Budget should annually report to the President on the implementation of this standard. All networks carrying classified data, including those in contractor corporations, should be subject to a Network Continuous Monitoring Program, similar to the EINSTEIN 3 and TUTELAGE programs, to record network traffic for real time and subsequent review to detect anomalous activity, malicious actions, and data breaches.

Recommendation 43

We recommend that the President's prior directions to improve the security of classified networks, Executive Order 13587, should be fully implemented as soon as possible.

Recommendation 44

We recommend that the National Security Council Principals Committee should annually meet to review the state of security of US Government networks carrying classified information, programs to improve such security, and evolving threats to such networks. An interagency "Red Team" should report annually to the Principals with an independent, "second opinion" on the state of security of the classified information networks.

Recommendation 45

We recommend that all US agencies and departments with classified information should expand their use of software, hardware, and procedures that limit access to documents and data to those specifically authorized to have access to them. The US Government should fund the development of, procure, and widely use on classified networks improved Information Rights Management software to control the dissemination of classified data in a way that provides greater restrictions on access and use, as well as an audit trail of such use.

Recommendation 46

We recommend the use of cost-benefit analysis and risk- management approaches, both prospective and retrospective, to orient judgments about personnel security and network security measures.

SECTION I. PRINCIPLES

1. The United States Government must protect, at once, two different forms of security: national security and personal privacy.

In the American tradition, the word "security" has had multiple meanings. In contemporary parlance, it often refers to *national security* or *homeland security*. Thus understood, it signals the immense importance of counteracting threats that come from those who seek to do the nation and its citizens harm. One of the government's most fundamental responsibilities is to protect this form of security, broadly understood. Appropriately conducted and properly disciplined, surveillance can help to eliminate important national security risks. It has helped to save lives in the past. It will help to do so in the future.

In the aftermath of the terrorist attacks of September 11, 2001, it should not be necessary to belabor this point. By their very nature, terrorist attacks tend to involve covert, decentralized actors who participate in plots that may not be easy to identify or disrupt. Surveillance can protect, and has protected, against such plots. But protection of national security includes a series of additional goals, prominently including counter- intelligence and counter-proliferation. It also includes support for military operations. Amidst serious military conflicts, surveillance can be an indispensable means of protecting the lives of those who serve or fight for our nation, and also (and it is important to emphasize this point) for our friends and allies.

At the same time, the idea of security refers to a quite different and equally fundamental value, captured in the Fourth Amendment to the United States Constitution: "The right of the people to be *secure* in their persons, houses, papers, and effects, against unreasonable searches and seizures, shall not be violated... ." (emphasis added). This form of security is a central component of the right of privacy, which Supreme Court Justice Louis Brandeis famously described as "the right to be let alone—the most comprehensive of rights and the right most valued by civilized men."[1] As Brandeis wrote, "The makers of our Constitution undertook to secure conditions favorable to the pursuit of happiness. They recognized the significance of man's spiritual nature, of his feelings, and of his intellect... . They sought to protect Americans in their beliefs, their thoughts, their emotions and their sensations."[2]

This protection is indispensable to the protection of security, properly conceived. In a free society, one that is genuinely committed to self- government, people are secure in the sense that they need not fear that their conversations and activities are being watched, monitored, questioned, interrogated, or scrutinized. Citizens are free from this kind of fear. In unfree societies, by contrast, there is no right to be let alone, and people struggle to organize their lives to avoid the government's probing eye. The resulting unfreedom jeopardizes, all at once, individual liberty, self-government, economic growth, and basic ideals of citizenship.

It might seem puzzling, or a coincidence of language, that the word "security" embodies such different values. But the etymology of the word solves the puzzle; there is no coincidence here. In Latin, the word "securus" offers the core meanings, which include "free from care, quiet, easy," and also "tranquil; free from danger, safe." People who are at physical risk because of a threat of external violence are by definition in danger; they are not safe. So too, people made insecure by their own government, in their persons, houses, papers, and effects, can hardly be "free from care" or "tranquil." And indeed, the first sentence of the Constitution juxtaposes the two values, explicitly using the word "secure":

> "We the People of the United States, in Order to form a more perfect Union, establish Justice, insure domestic Tranquility, *provide for the common defense*, promote the general Welfare, and *secure the Blessings of Liberty to ourselves and our Posterity*, do ordain and establish this Constitution for the United States of America" (emphasis added).

Some people believe that the two forms of security are in irreconcilable conflict with one another. They contend that in the modern era, with serious threats to the homeland and the rise of modern communications technologies, the nation must choose between them. We firmly reject this view. It is unsupported by the facts. It is inconsistent with our traditions and our law. Free societies can and must take the necessary steps to protect national security, by enabling public officials to counteract and to anticipate genuine threats, while also ensuring that the people are secure "in their persons, houses, papers, and effects."

2. The central task is one of risk management; multiple risks are involved, and all of them must be considered.

When public officials acquire information, they seek to reduce risks, above all risks to national security. If the government is able to obtain access to a great deal of information, it should be in a better position to mitigate serious threats of violence. And if the goal is to reduce such threats, a wide net seems far better than a narrow one, even if the government ends up acquiring a great deal of information that it does not need or want. As technologies evolve, it is becoming increasingly feasible to cast that wide net. In the future, the feasibility of pervasive surveillance will increase dramatically. From the standpoint of risk reduction, that prospect has real advantages.

The challenge, of course, is that multiple risks are involved. The government must consider all of those risks, not a subset, when it is creating sensible safeguards. In addition to reducing risks to national security, public officials must consider four other risks.

Risks to privacy. It is self-evident that as more information is acquired, the risk to privacy increases as well. One reason is that officials might obtain personal or private information that has nothing to do with threats of violence or indeed with criminality at all. History shows that the acquisition of information can create risks of misuse and abuse, perhaps in the form of intrusion into a legitimately private sphere. History also shows that when government is engaged in surveillance, it can undermine public trust, and in that sense render its own citizens insecure. Privacy is a central aspect of liberty, and it must be safeguarded.

Risks to freedom and civil liberties on the Internet and elsewhere. Liberty includes a range of values, such as freedom of speech, freedom of religion, and freedom of association, that go well beyond privacy. If people are fearful that their conversations are being monitored, expressions of doubt about or opposition to current policies and leaders may be chilled, and the democratic process itself may be compromised.

Along with many other nations, the United States has been committed to the preservation and expansion of the Internet as an open, global space for freedom of expression. The pursuit of Internet freedom represents the effort to protect human rights online. These rights include the right to speak out, to dissent, and to offer or receive information across national borders. Citizens ought to be able to enjoy these rights, free from fear that their words will result in punishment or threat. A particular concern involves preservation of the rights, and the security, of journalists and the press; their rights and their security are indispensable to self-government.

Risks to our relationships with other nations. Insofar as the information comes from other nations—whether their leaders or their citizens—its acquisition, dissemination, or use might seriously compromise our relationships with those very nations. It is important to consider the potential effects of surveillance on these relationships and, in particular, on our close allies and others with whom we share values, interests, or both. Unnecessary or excessive surveillance can create risks that outweigh any gain. Those who do not live within our borders should be treated with dignity and respect, and an absence of such treatment can create real risks.

Risks to trade and commerce, including international commerce. Free trade, including free communications, is important to commerce and economic growth. Surveillance and the acquisition of information might have harmful effects on commerce, especially if it discourages people— either citizens of the United States or others—from using certain communications providers. If the government is working closely or secretly with specific providers, and if such providers cannot assure their users that their communications are safe and secure, people might well look elsewhere. In principle, the economic damage could be severe.

These points make it abundantly clear that if officials *can* acquire information, it does not follow that they *should* do so. Indeed, the fact that officials can *legally* acquire information (under domestic law) does not mean that they should do so. In view of growing technological capacities, and the possibility (however remote) that acquired information might prove useful, it is tempting to think that such capacities should be used rather than ignored. The temptation should be resisted. Officials must consider all relevant risks, not merely one or a subset.

To this point we add an additional consideration, which is the immense importance of maintaining public trust. Some reforms are justified as improvements of the system of risk management. Other reforms are justified, not only or primarily on that ground, but as ways to promote a general sense, in the United States and abroad, that the nation's practices and decisions are worthy of trust.

3. The idea of "balancing" has an important element of truth, but it is also inadequate and misleading.

It is tempting to suggest that the underlying goal is to achieve the right "balance" between the two forms of security. The suggestion has an important element of truth. Some tradeoffs are inevitable; we shall explore the question of balance in some detail. But in critical respects, the suggestion is inadequate and misleading.

Some safeguards are not subject to balancing at all. In a free society, public officials should never engage in surveillance in order to punish their political enemies; to restrict freedom of speech or religion; to suppress legitimate criticism and dissent; to help their preferred companies or industries; to provide domestic companies with an unfair competitive advantage; or to benefit or burden members of groups defined in terms of religion, ethnicity, race, or gender. These prohibitions are foundational, and they apply both inside and outside our territorial borders.

The purposes of surveillance must be legitimate. If they are not, no amount of "balancing" can justify surveillance. For this reason, it is exceptionally important to create explicit prohibitions and safeguards, designed to reduce the risk that surveillance will ever be undertaken for illegitimate ends.

4. The government should base its decisions on a careful analysis of consequences, including both benefits and costs (to the extent feasible).

In many areas of policy, public officials are increasingly insistent on the need for careful analysis of the consequences of their decisions and on the importance of relying not on intuitions and anecdotes, but on evidence and data, including benefits and costs (to the extent feasible). In the context of government regulation, President Ronald Reagan established a national commitment to careful analysis of regulations in his Executive Order 12291, issued in 1981. In 2011, President Barack Obama issued Executive Order 13563, which renewed and deepened the commitment to quantitative, evidence-based analysis, and added a number of additional requirements to improve regulatory review, directing agencies "to use the best available techniques to quantify anticipated present and future benefits and costs as accurately as possible" in order to achieve regulatory ends.

A central component of Executive Order 13563 involves "retrospective analysis," meant to ensure not merely prospective analysis of (anticipated) costs and benefits, but also continuing efforts to explore what policies have actually achieved, or failed to achieve, in the real world. In our view, both prospective and retrospective analyses have important roles to play in the domain under discussion, though they also present distinctive challenges, above all because of limits in available knowledge and challenges in quantifying certain variables.

Before they are undertaken, surveillance decisions should depend (to the extent feasible) on a careful assessment of the anticipated consequences, including the full range of relevant risks. Such decisions should also be subject to continuing scrutiny, including retrospective analysis, to ensure that any errors are corrected.

As we have seen, there is always a possibility that acquisition of more information—whether in the US or abroad—might ultimately prove helpful. But that abstract possibility does not, by itself, provide a sufficient justification for acquiring more information. Because risk management is inevitably involved, the question is one of benefits and costs, which requires careful attention to the range of possible outcomes and also to the likelihood that they will actually occur. To the extent feasible, such attention must be based on the available evidence.

Where evidence is unavailable, public officials must acknowledge the limits of what they know. In some cases, public officials are reasonably attempting to reduce risks that are not subject to specification or quantification in advance. In such cases, experience may turn out to be the best teacher; it may show that programs are not working well, and that the benefits and costs are different from what was anticipated. Continued learning and constant scrutiny, with close reference to the consequences, is necessary to safeguard both national security and personal privacy, and to ensure proper management of the full range of risks that are involved.

Finally, in constructing oversight and monitoring of intelligence agencies and particularly of surveillance, the US Government must take care to address perceptions of potential abuse, as well as any realities. To maintain and enhance the required level of public trust, especially careful oversight is advisable.

SECTION II. LESSONS OF HISTORY

A. The Continuing Challenge

For reasons that we have outlined, it is always challenging to strike the right balance between the often competing values of national security and individual liberty, but as history teaches, it is *particularly* difficult to reconcile these values in times of real or perceived national crisis. Human nature being what it is, there is inevitably a risk of overreaction when we act out of fear. At such moments, those charged with the responsibility for keeping our nation safe, supported by an anxious public, have too often gone beyond programs and policies that were in fact necessary and appropriate to protect the nation and taken steps that unnecessarily and sometimes dangerously jeopardized individual freedom.

This phenomenon is evident throughout American history. Too often, we have overreacted in periods of national crisis and then later, with the benefit of hindsight, recognized our failures, reevaluated our judgments, and attempted to correct our policies going forward. We must learn the lessons of history.

As early as 1798, Congress enacted the Sedition Act, now widely regarded as a violation of the most fundamental principles of freedom of expression. Nor is the historical verdict kind to a wide range of liberty- restricting measures undertaken in other periods of great national anxiety, including the repeated suspensions of the writ of habeas corpus during the Civil War, the suppression of dissent during World War I, the internment of Japanese-Americans during World War II, the campaign to expose and harass persons suspected of "disloyalty" during the McCarthy era, and the widespread and unlawful spying on critics of the government's policies during the Vietnam War.[3]

It is true that when the nation is at risk, or engaged in some kind of military conflict, the argument for new restrictions may seem, and even be, plausible. Serious threats may tip preexisting balances. But it is also true that in such periods, there is a temptation to ignore the fact that risks are on all sides of the equation, and to compromise liberty at the expense of security. One of our central goals in this Report is to provide secure foundations for future decisions, when public fears may heighten those dangers.

With respect to surveillance in particular, the nation's history is lengthy and elaborate, but the issues in the modern era can be traced back directly to the Vietnam War. Presidents Lyndon Johnson and Richard Nixon encouraged government intelligence agencies to investigate alleged "subversives" in the antiwar movement. The Federal Bureau of Investigation (FBI) engaged in extensive infiltration and electronic surveillance of individuals and organizations opposed to the war; the Central Intelligence Agency (CIA) monitored a broad array of antiwar organizations and activities, accumulating information on more than 300,000 people; and Army intelligence initiated its own domestic spying operation, gathering information on more than 100,000 opponents of the Vietnam War, including Members of Congress, civil rights leaders, and journalists. The government sought not only to investigate its critics on a massive scale, but also to expose, disrupt, and neutralize their efforts to affect public opinion.[4]

As some of this information came to light, Congress authorized investigating committees to probe more deeply. One Senate committee made the following findings:

> The Government has often undertaken the secret surveillance of citizens on the basis of their political beliefs, even when those beliefs posed no threat of violence or illegal acts... . The Government, operating primarily through secret informants, ... has swept in vast amounts of information about the personal lives, views, and associations of American citizens. Investigations of groups deemed potentially dangerous—and even of groups suspected of associating with potentially dangerous organizations—have continued for decades, despite the fact that those groups did not engage in unlawful activity[5]... .

In 1976, President Gerald Ford formally prohibited the CIA from using electronic or physical surveillance to collect information about the domestic activities of Americans and banned the National Security Agency from intercepting any communication made within, from, or to the United States, except lawful electronic surveillance under procedures approved by the Attorney General.[6] That same year, Attorney General Edward Levi imposed new restrictions on the investigative activities of the FBI. In these guidelines, the Attorney General prohibited the FBI from investigating any group or individual on the basis of protected First Amendment activity in the absence of "specific and articulable facts" justifying a criminal investigation. Attorney General Levi adopted these guidelines without regard to whether such investigations violated the Constitution. He justified them as sound public policy and contended that the protection of civil liberties demands not only compliance with the Constitution, but also a restrained use of government power, undertaking what we would describe as a form of risk management. [7]

The United States has made great progress over time in its protection of "the Blessings of Liberty"—even in times of crisis. The major restrictions of civil liberties that have blackened our past would be unthinkable today. This is an important national achievement, and one we should not take for granted. But it is much easier to look back on past crises and find our predecessors wanting than it is to make wise judgments when we ourselves are in the eye of the storm. As time passes, new dangers, new technologies, and new threats to our freedom continually emerge. Knowing what we did right—and wrong—in the past is a useful, indeed indispensable, guide, but it does not tell us how to get it right in the future. One of the central goals of this Report is to suggest reforms that will reduce the risk of overreaction in the future.

B. The Legal Framework as of September 11, 2001

In the wake of the disclosures in the 1970s, several congressional committees examined the failures that led to the abuses. The most influential of those committees was the Senate's Select Committee to Study Governmental Operations with Respect to Intelligence Activities, which issued its comprehensive Final Report in April of 1976. Known as the Church Committee, after its chairman, Senator Frank Church, this Report has shaped much of our nation's thinking about foreign intelligence surveillance for the past 40 years[8]

At the outset, the Committee stated unequivocally that espionage, sabotage, and terrorist acts "can seriously endanger" both the security of the nation and "the rights of Americans," that "carefully focused intelligence investigations can help prevent such acts," and that "properly controlled and lawful intelligence is vital to the nation's interest." At the same time, the Committee emphasized the dangers that "intelligence collection ... may pose for a society grounded in democratic principles." Echoing former Attorney General and Supreme Court Chief Justice Harlan Fiske Stone, the Committee warned that an intelligence agency operating in secret can "become a menace to a free government ... because it carries with it the possibility of abuses of power which are not always quickly apprehended or understood." The "critical question," the Committee explained, is "to determine how the fundamental liberties of the people can be maintained in the course of the Government's effort to protect their security."[9]

Looking back over the preceding decades, the Committee noted that "too often ... intelligence activities have invaded individual privacy and violated the rights of lawful assembly and political expression."[10] This danger, the Committee observed, is inherent in the very essence of government intelligence programs, because the "natural tendency of Government is toward abuse of power" and because "men entrusted with power, even those aware of its dangers, tend, particularly when pressured, to slight liberty."[11] Moreover, because abuse thrives on secrecy, there is a natural "tendency of intelligence activities to expand beyond their initial scope" and to "generate ever-increasing demands for new data."[12] And to make matters worse, "once intelligence has been collected there are strong pressures to use it."[13]

In reviewing "the overwhelming ... excesses" of the past, the Church Committee found not only that those excesses violated the rights of Americans by invading their privacy and "undermining the democratic process," but also that their "usefulness" in "serving the legitimate goal of protecting society" was often "questionable."[14] Those abuses, the Committee reasoned, "were due in large measure to the fact that the system of checks and balances—created in our Constitution to limit abuse of Governmental power—was seldom applied to the Intelligence Community."[15]

The absence of checks and balances occurred both because government officials failed to exercise appropriate oversight and because intelligence agencies systematically concealed "improper activities from their superiors in the Executive branch and from the Congress."[16] Although recognizing that "the excesses of the past do not ... justify depriving the United States" of the capacity to "anticipate" and prevent "terrorist violence," the Committee made clear that "clear legal standards and effective oversight are necessary to ensure" that "intelligence activity does not itself undermine the democratic system it is intended to protect."[17]

In looking to the future, the Committee was especially concerned with the impact of new and emerging technologies. The Committee expressly invoked Justice Louis Brandeis' famous dissenting opinion in *Olmstead v. United States*,[18] in which the Supreme Court held in 1928, over the objections of Justices Brandeis and Oliver Wendell Holmes, that wiretapping was not a "search" within the meaning of the Fourth Amendment. In his dissenting opinion, Justice Brandeis cautioned that, since the adoption of the Constitution, "subtler and more far-reaching means of invading privacy have become available to the government ... [and] the progress of science in furnishing the Government with means of espionage is not likely to stop with wiretapping."[19] The Committee observed that Brandeis' warning applied "with obvious force to the technological developments that allow NSA to monitor an enormous number of communications each year."[20]

"Personal privacy," the Committee added, is "essential to liberty and the pursuit of happiness" and is necessary to ensure "that all our citizens may live in a free and decent society."[21] Indeed, "when Government infringes the right of privacy, the injury spreads far beyond the particular citizens targeted to untold numbers of other Americans who may be intimidated." The Committee added that, in the words of former Attorney General and Supreme Court Justice Robert H. Jackson, without clear legal limitations, "a federal investigative agency would 'have enough on enough people' so that 'even if it does not elect to prosecute them' the Government would ... still 'find no opposition to its policies.'"[22] Indeed, Jackson added, "even those who are supposed to supervise [our intelligence agencies] are likely to fear [them].'"[23]

With this warning in mind, the Committee cautioned that, "in an era where the technological capability of Government relentlessly increases, we must be wary about the drift toward 'big brother government.'" Because "the potential for abuse is awesome," it demands "special attention to fashioning restraints which not only cure past problems but anticipate and prevent the future misuse of technology." To this end, "those within the Executive Branch and the Congress ... must be fully informed" if they are to "exercise their responsibilities wisely." Moreover, "the American public ... should know enough about intelligence activities to be able to apply its good sense to the underlying issues of policy and morality." "Knowledge," the Committee insisted, "is the key to control." Thus, "secrecy should no longer be allowed to shield the existence of constitutional, legal, and moral problems from the scrutiny of the three branches of government or from the American people themselves."[24]

The Committee called for "a comprehensive legislative charter defining and controlling the intelligence activities of the Federal Government."[25] The Committee set forth a series of specific principles and recommendations, including the following:

- "There is no inherent constitutional authority for the President or any intelligence agency to violate the law."
- "Government action which directly infringes the rights of free speech and association must be prohibited."
- "No intelligence agency may engage" in "federal domestic security activities ... unless authorized by statute."

- The NSA "should not monitor domestic communications, even for foreign intelligence purposes."
- To the extent the NSA inadvertently monitors the communications of Americans, it must "make every practicable effort to eliminate or minimize the extent to which the communications are intercepted, selected, or monitored."
- To the extent the NSA inadvertently monitors the communications of Americans, it should be prohibited "from disseminating such communications, or information derived therefrom, ... unless the communication indicates evidence of hostile foreign intelligence or terrorist activity, or felonious criminal conduct, or contains a threat of death or serious bodily harm."
- "NSA should not request from any communications carrier any communication which it could not otherwise obtain pursuant to these recommendations."
- "The responsibility and authority of the Attorney General for oversight of federal domestic security activities must be clarified and general counsels and inspectors general of intelligence agencies strengthened."
- "Each year the ... intelligence agencies ... should be required to seek annual statutory authorization for their programs."
- Congress should establish a "scheme which will afford effective redress to people who are injured by improper federal intelligence activity."
- There should be "vigorous" congressional "oversight to review the conduct of domestic security activities through new permanent intelligence oversight committees."
- Because "American citizens should not lose their constitutional rights to be free from improper intrusion by their Government when they travel overseas," the "rights of Americans" must be protected "abroad as well as at home."[26]

In 1978, Congress enacted the Foreign Intelligence Surveillance Act (FISA) to implement the recommendations of the Church Committee and other congressional committees.[27] A central issue concerned the legality of electronic surveillance for the purpose of foreign intelligence. In 1928, the Supreme Court had held in *Olmstead*[28] that a wiretap is not a "search" within the meaning of the Fourth Amendment because it does not involve a *physical* intrusion into an individual's personal property. Despite the holding in *Olmstead*, in the 1934 Communications Act Congress limited the circumstances in which government officials could lawfully engage in wiretaps in the context of criminal investigations.[29]

In 1967, in *Katz v. United States*,[30] the Court overruled *Olmstead*, noting that the Fourth Amendment "protects people not places." The Court reasoned that, in light of the realities of modern technology, the Fourth Amendment must be understood to protect the individual's and society's "reasonable expectations of privacy." It was this holding that led to the conclusion that the Fourth Amendment prohibits the government from using wiretapping unless it first obtains a search warrant from a neutral and detached magistrate based on a finding of probable cause to believe that the interception will produce evidence of criminal conduct.

It remained unclear, however, whether that same rule would apply when the government investigates "the activities of *foreign powers*, within or without this country."[31] The general assumption was that the President has broad constitutional authority to protect the nation in the realm of foreign intelligence surveillance without complying with the usual requirements of the Fourth Amendment. It was against this background that Congress considered FISA.

FISA attempted to safeguard the nation against the kinds of abuses that had been documented by the Church Committee, while at the same time preserving the nation's ability to protect itself against external threats. FISA was a carefully designed compromise between those who wanted to preserve maximum flexibility for the intelligence agencies and those who wanted to place foreign intelligence surveillance under essentially the same restrictions as ordinary surveillance activities (at least insofar as the rights of Americans were concerned).

To that end, FISA brought foreign intelligence surveillance within a legal regime involving strict rules and structured oversight by all three branches of the government, but also granted the government greater freedom in the realm of foreign intelligence surveillance than it had in the context of others types of surveillance.[32]

FISA restricted the government's authority to use electronic surveillance *inside the United States* to obtain foreign intelligence from "foreign powers." The term "foreign powers" was defined to include not only foreign nations, but also the agents of foreign nations and any "group engaged in international terrorism."[33] FISA established the Foreign Intelligence Surveillance Court (FISC), consisting of seven (now eleven) federal judges appointed by the Chief Justice of the United States to serve staggered terms on the FISC. FISA provided that any government agency seeking to use electronic surveillance for foreign intelligence purposes inside the United States had to obtain a warrant from the FISC. For such a warrant to be issued, the government had to show "probable cause to believe that the target of the electronic surveillance" is an agent of a foreign power.[34]

It is important to note several significant elements to this approach. First, by requiring the government to obtain a warrant from the FISC, FISA denied the President the previously assumed authority to engage in foreign intelligence surveillance inside the United States without judicial supervision. This was a major innovation.

Second, Congress created the FISC so it could deal with classified information and programs involved in foreign intelligence surveillance. Ordinary federal courts lacked the facilities and clearances to deal with such matters. A special court was therefore necessary if such classified matters were to be brought under the rule of law.

Third, FISA did not deal with the President's authority to engage in foreign intelligence activities *outside the United States*. FISA did not require the government to obtain a FISA warrant from the FISC before it could legally wiretap a telephone conversation between two Russians in Moscow or between a US citizen in France and a US citizen in England. In such circumstances, FISA left the issue, as in the past, to the Executive Branch, operating under the National Security Act of 1947,[35] the National Security Agency Act of 1959,[36] and the US Constitution.

Fourth, FISA did not limit the government's use of electronic surveillance in the foreign intelligence context to those situations in which the government has probable cause to believe that criminal activity is afoot. Rather, FISA permitted the government to engage in electronic surveillance in the United States to obtain foreign intelligence information as long as the government can establish to the satisfaction of the FISC that it has probable cause to believe that the "target" of the surveillance is an "agent of a foreign power."

These features of the system established by FISA reflect Congress' understanding at the time of the central differences between electronic surveillance for foreign intelligence purposes and electronic surveillance for traditional criminal investigation purposes. But in light of past abuses, the possibility of politicization, and the decision to authorize foreign intelligence surveillance of individuals, including American citizens, for whom there is no probable cause to suspect criminal conduct, FISA instituted a broad range of safeguards to prevent misuse of this authority.

For example, FISA requires the Attorney General to approve all applications for FISA warrants; it requires the Attorney General to report to the House and Senate Intelligence Committees every six months on the FISA process and the results of FISA-authorized surveillance; it requires the Attorney General to make an annual report to Congress and the public about the total number of applications made for FISA warrants and the total number of applications granted, modified, or denied; and it expressly provides that no United States citizen or legal resident of the United States may be targeted for surveillance under FISA "solely upon the basis of activities protected by the first amendment to the Constitution of the United States." Finally, FISA requires the use of "minimization" procedures to protect the privacy rights of individuals who are not themselves "targets" of FISA surveillance but whose conversations or personal information are *incidentally* picked up in the course of electronic surveillance of legitimate targets under the Act.[37]

FISA changed only modestly from 1978 until the events of September 11, 2001. Although FISA originally applied only to electronic surveillance, Congress gradually widened its scope to other methods of investigation. In 1995, it was extended to physical searches; in 1998, it was extended to pen register and trap-and-trace orders (which enable the government to obtain lists of the telephone numbers and e-mails contacted by an individual after the issuance of the order); and in that same year it was extended to permit access to limited forms of business records, including documents kept by common carriers, public accommodation facilities, storage facilities, and vehicle rental facilities.[38]

From 1978 until 2001, FISA offered an important legal framework designed to maintain the balance between the nation's commitment both to "provide for the common defence" and to "secure the Blessings of Liberty."

FISA is not the only legal authority governing foreign intelligence activities. Other statutes and Executive Orders address other facets of the operations of the Intelligence Community. The National Security Act[39] and other laws relating to specific agencies, such as the Central Intelligence Agency Act[40] and the National Security Agency Act,[41] regulate what agencies can do, and the Intelligence Community is also governed by laws such as the Privacy Act[42] and the Electronic Communications Privacy Act.[43]

Executive Order 12333 is the principal Executive Branch authority for foreign intelligence activities *not governed by FISA*.[44] Executive Order 12333 specifies the missions and authorities of each element of the Intelligence Community; sets forth the principles designed to strike an appropriate balance between the acquisition of information and the protection of personal privacy; and governs the collection, retention, and dissemination of information about United States Persons (American citizens and non- citizens who are legal residents of the United States).

Executive Order 12333 authorizes the Attorney General to promulgate guidelines requiring each element of the Intelligence Community to have in place procedures prescribing how it can collect, retain, and disseminate information about US persons. The guidelines define each agency's authorities and responsibilities. With respect to National Security Agency (NSA), for example, Executive Order 12333 designates NSA as the manager for Signals Intelligence (SIGINT) for the Intelligence Community, and the Attorney General's Guidelines define how SIGINT may be conducted for collection activities not governed by FISA.[45]

Section 2.4 of Executive Order 12333 prohibits specific elements of the Intelligence Community from engaging in certain types of activities inside the United States. The CIA, for example, is generally prohibited from engaging in electronic surveillance, and members of the Intelligence Community other than the FBI are generally prohibited from conducting non-consensual physical searches inside the United States.

As the principal governing authority for United States intelligence activities *outside the United States*, Executive Order 12333 requires that the collection of foreign intelligence information conform to established intelligence priorities. Under this authority, electronic surveillance of non- US Persons who are outside the United States must meet a separate set of standards. These standards and priorities are discussed in Section IV of this Report.

C. September 11 and Its Aftermath

The September 11 attacks were a vivid demonstration of the need for detailed information about the activities of potential terrorists. This was so for several reasons.

First, some information, which could have been useful, was not collected and other information, which could have helped to prevent the attacks, was not shared among departments.

Second, the scale of damage that 21st-century terrorists can inflict is far greater than anything that their predecessors could have imagined. We are no longer dealing with threats from firearms and conventional explosives, but with the possibility of weapons of mass destruction, including nuclear devices and biological and chemical agents. The damage that such attacks could inflict on the nation, measured in terms of loss of life, economic and social disruption, and the consequent sacrifice of civil liberties, is extraordinary. The events of September 11 brought this home with crystal clarity.

Third, 21st-century terrorists operate within a global communications network that enables them both to hide their existence from outsiders and to communicate with one another across continents at the speed of light. Effective safeguards against terrorist attacks require the technological capacity to ferret out such communications in an international communications grid.

Fourth, many of the international terrorists that the United States and other nations confront today cannot realistically be deterred by the fear of punishment. The conventional means of preventing criminal conduct—the fear of capture and subsequent punishment—has relatively little role to play in combating some contemporary terrorists. Unlike the situation during the Cold War, in which the Soviet Union was deterred from launching a nuclear strike against the United States in part by its fear of a retaliatory counterattack, the terrorist enemy in the 21st-century is not a nation state against which the United States and its allies can retaliate with the same effectiveness. In such circumstances, detection in advance is essential in any effort to "provide for the common defence."

Fifth, the threat of massive terrorist attacks involving nuclear, chemical, or biological weapons can generate a chilling and destructive environment of fear and anxiety among our nation's citizens. If Americans came to believe that we are infiltrated by enemies we cannot identify and who have the power to bring death, destruction, and chaos to our lives on a massive scale, and that preventing such attacks is beyond the capacity of our government, the quality of national life would be greatly imperiled. Indeed, if a similar or even more devastating attack were to occur in the future, there would almost surely be an impulse to increase the use of surveillance technology to prevent further strikes, despite the potentially corrosive effects on individual freedom and self-governance.

In the years after the attacks of September 11, a former cabinet member suggested a vivid analogy. He compared "the task of stopping" the next terrorist attack "to a goalie in a soccer game who 'must stop every shot,'" for if the enemy "'scores a single goal,'" the terrorists succeed. To make matters worse, "'the goalie cannot see the ball—it is invisible. So are the players—he doesn't know how many there are, or where they are, or what they look like.'"[46] Indeed, the invisible players might shoot the ball "from the front of the goal, or from the back, or from some other direction—the goalie just doesn't know.'"[47]

Although the analogy might be overstated, it is no surprise that after the September 11, 2001 terrorist attacks the government turned to a much more aggressive form of surveillance in an effort to locate and identify potential terrorists and prevent future attacks before they could occur. One thing seemed clear: If the government was overly cautious in its efforts to detect and prevent terrorist attacks, the consequences for the nation could be disastrous. The challenge was, and remains, how to obtain information without compromising other values, including the freedoms that Americans, and citizens of many other nations, hold most dear.

D. The Intelligence Community

Executive Order 12333 sets forth the central objective of the nation's Intelligence Community: "Accurate and timely information about the capabilities, intentions and activities of foreign powers, organizations or persons and their agents is essential to informed decisionmaking in the areas of national defense and foreign relations. Collection of such information is a priority objective and will be pursued in a vigorous, innovative and responsible manner that is consistent with the Constitution and applicable law and respectful of the principles upon which the United States was founded."[48] Although the Review Group was not charged with the task of undertaking a comprehensive evaluation of all of the many and varied elements and activities of the Intelligence Community, we can offer a few general observations.

First, the collection of foreign intelligence is a vital component of protecting the national security, including protection from terrorist threats. Indeed, foreign intelligence may be more important today than ever before in our history. This is so in part because the number of significant national security and foreign policy issues facing the United States in the 21st century is large and perhaps unprecedented. These issues include the threats of international terrorism, the proliferation of weapons of mass destruction, cyber espionage and warfare, the risk of mass atrocities, and the international elements of organized crime and narcotics and human trafficking. They include as well the challenges associated with winding down the war in Afghanistan, profound and revolutionary change in the Middle East, and successfully managing our critically important relationships with China and Russia.

Most of these challenges have a significant intelligence component. Policymakers cannot understand the issues, cannot make policy with regard to those issues, and cannot successfully implement that policy without reliable intelligence. Any expert with access to open sources can provide insight on questions such as the Eurozone crisis and Japanese politics, but insights on the plans, intentions, and capabilities of al-Qa'ida, on the status of the Iranian nuclear weapons program, and on the development of cyber warfare tools by other nations are simply not possible without reliable intelligence.

A wide range of intelligence collectors, including NSA, have made important contributions to protecting the nation's security. Notwithstanding recent controversies, and the importance of significant reforms, the national security of the United States depends on the continued capacity of NSA and other agencies to collect essential information. In considering proposals for reform, now and for the future, policymakers should avoid the risk of overreaction and take care in making changes that could undermine the capabilities of the Intelligence Community.

Second, although recent disclosures and commentary have created the impression in some quarters that NSA surveillance is indiscriminate and pervasive across the globe, that is not the case. NSA focuses on collecting foreign intelligence information that is relevant to protecting the national security of the United States and its allies. Moreover, much of what NSA collects is shared with the governments of many other nations for the purpose of enhancing their national security and the personal security of their citizens.

Third, FISA put in place a system of oversight, review, and checks- and-balances to reduce the risk that elements of the Intelligence Community would operate outside of the law. We offer many recommendations to improve the existing procedures, but it is important to note that they now include a wide range of inspectors general, privacy oversight boards, minimization procedures,[49] intensive training requirements, mandatory reviews by the Attorney General and the Director of National Intelligence, judicial oversight by the FISA Court, and regular reporting to Congress. Appendix C provides information on these oversight mechanisms.

Significantly, and in stark contrast to the pre-FISA era, the Review Group found no evidence of illegality or other abuse of authority for the purpose of targeting domestic political activity. This is of central importance, because one of the greatest dangers of government surveillance is the potential to use what is learned to undermine democratic governance. On the other hand, as discussed later in this Report, there have been serious and persistent instances of noncompliance in the Intelligence Community's implementation of its authorities. Even if unintentional, these instances of noncompliance raise serious concerns about the Intelligence Community's capacity to manage its authorities in an effective and lawful manner.

Fourth, many of the rules governing the actions of the Intelligence Community were amended in the wake of the attacks of September 11. Predictably, and quite properly, they were amended to give the Intelligence Community much broader authority to take action to ensure that the United States could prevent similar attacks in the future. But because we were acting in a moment of crisis, there was always the risk that the new rules—and the new authorities granted to the Intelligence Community—might have gone too far.

It is now time to step back and take stock. With the benefit of experience, and as detailed below, we conclude that some of the authorities that were expanded or created in the aftermath of September 11 unduly sacrifice fundamental interests in individual liberty, personal privacy, and democratic governance. We believe that our recommended modifications of those authorities strike a better balance between the competing interests in providing for the common defense and securing "the Blessings of Liberty to ourselves and our Posterity."

We make these recommendations with a profound sense of caution, humility, and respect, and with full awareness that they will require careful deliberation and close attention to consequences. There is no doubt that the degree of safety and security our nation has enjoyed in the years since September 11 has been made possible in no small part by the energetic, determined, and effective actions of the Intelligence Community. For that, all Americans should be both proud and grateful. But even that degree of success does not mean that we cannot strike a better balance for the future.

SECTION III. REFORMING FOREIGN INTELLIGENCE SURVEILLANCE DIRECTED AT UNITED STATES PERSONS

A. Introduction

A central concern of this Report is the need to define an appropriate balance between protecting the privacy interests of United States persons and protecting the nation's security. In this section, we focus primarily on section 215 of FISA and related issues, such as the FBI's use of national security letters, because those issues have received particular attention in recent months as a result of disclosures relating to business records.

The central issue concerns the authority of the government in general, and the Intelligence Community in particular, to require third- parties, such as telephone and Internet companies, to turn over their business records to the government. Because the data contained in those records can reveal significant information about the private lives of United States persons, it is essential to think carefully about the circumstances in which the government should have access to those records.

This section also deals with the collection of business records containing meta-data. To what extent does the disclosure of information about the telephone numbers or e-mails an individual contacts, which constitute meta-data, implicate significant privacy interests? In addition, this section offers recommendations addressing more general questions about transparency and secrecy in the activities of the Intelligence Community. A central goal of our recommendations is to increase transparency and to decrease unnecessary secrecy, in order to enhance both accountability and public trust.

B. Section 215: Background

Only a week after the September 11 terrorist attacks, the Bush Administration proposed the PATRIOT Act to Congress. That legislation, which was adopted by an overwhelming vote, made several significant changes in FISA.[50] Among the most important was the addition of section 215, which substantially expanded the scope of permissible FISA orders to compel third parties to turn over to the government business records and other tangible objects.

As originally enacted in 1978, FISA did not grant the government any authority to compel the production of such records. In 1998, however, after the Oklahoma City and first World Trade Center bombings, Congress amended FISA to authorize the FISC to issue orders compelling the production of a narrow set of records from "a common carrier, public accommodation facility, physical storage facility or vehicle rental facility" for use in "an investigation to gather foreign intelligence information or an investigation concerning international terrorism" upon a showing of "specific and articulable facts giving reason to believe that the person to whom the records pertain is a foreign power or an agent of a foreign power."[51]

Section 215 of the PATRIOT Act substantially expanded this authority in two important ways. First, it eliminated the limitation on the types of entities that could be compelled to produce these records and authorized the FISC to issue orders compelling the production of "any tangible things including books, records, papers, documents, and other items." Second, it changed the standard for the issuance of such orders. Instead of requiring the government to demonstrate that it has "specific and articulable facts giving reason to believe that the person to whom the records pertain is a foreign power or an agent of a foreign power,"[52] section 215 authorized the FISC to issue such orders whenever the government sought records for an authorized "investigation to protect against international terrorism or clandestine intelligence activities."[53]

This formulation was criticized as being too open-ended, however, and Congress thereafter amended section 215 in the USA PATRIOT Improvement and Reauthorization Act of 2005, which authorized the FISC to issue such orders only if the government provides "a statement of facts showing that there are reasonable grounds to believe that the tangible objects sought are relevant" to an authorized investigation intended to protect "against international terrorism or clandestine intelligence activities."[54]

Is section 215 consistent with the Fourth Amendment? There are two concerns. First, section 215 does not require a showing of probable cause. The Supreme Court has long held, however, that the "Fourth Amendment was not intended to interfere with the power of courts to compel, through a subpoena, the production" of evidence, as long as the order compelling the production of records or other tangible objects meets the general test of "reasonableness."[55] In theory, section 215 extends the principle of the subpoena from the traditional criminal investigation into the realm of foreign intelligence.

Second, in many instances section 215 is used to obtain records that implicate the privacy interests of individuals whose personal information is contained in records held by a third party. This is so, for example, when the government seeks to obtain financial information about a particular individual from her bank, or telephone calling data about a particular individual from her telephone company. In a series of decisions in the 1970s, the Supreme Court held that individuals have no "reasonable expectation of privacy" in information they voluntarily share with third parties, such as banks and telephone companies, explaining that "what a person knowingly exposes" to third parties "is not a subject of Fourth Amendment protection." In *Miller v. United States*[56] the Court applied this reasoning to bank records and in *Smith v. Maryland*[57] it extended it to an individual's telephone calling records.

Those decisions led to the enactment of section 215. In 1978, relying on *Miller* and *Smith*, Congress enacted the Right to Financial Privacy Act of 1978.[58] Although the Right to Financial Privacy Act generally prohibited financial institutions from disclosing personal financial records, it expressly authorized them to disclose such records in response to lawful subpoenas and search warrants.[59] In the national security context, Congress relied upon *Miller* and *Smith* to give the government important new tools to collect foreign intelligence information.

In 1998, for example, Congress amended FISA to grant the government "pen register" and "trap-and-trace" authority.[60] A trap-and- trace device identifies the sources of incoming calls and a pen register indicates the numbers called from a particular phone number. The 1998 amendment authorized the FISC to issue orders compelling telephone service providers to permit the government to install these devices upon a showing that the government seeks to obtain information "relevant" to a foreign intelligence investigation.[61]

That same year, as noted earlier, Congress enacted the precursor of section 215, which, as amended, authorizes the FISC to issue orders compelling the production of records and other tangible objects from third parties whenever the government has "reasonable grounds to believe" that the records or "objects sought are relevant" to an authorized investigation intended to protect "against international terrorism or clandestine intelligence activities."[62] The PATRIOT Act later expanded this authority to include sender/addressee information relating to e-mail and other forms of electronic communications.[63]

Although these authorities were made possible by *Miller* and *Smith*, there is some question today whether those decisions are still good law. In its 2012 decision in *United States v. Jones*,[64] the Court held that long-term surveillance of an individual's location effected by attaching a GPS device to his car constituted a trespass and therefore a "search" within the meaning of the Fourth Amendment. In reaching this result, five of the Justices suggested that the surveillance might have infringed on the driver's "reasonable expectations of privacy" even if there had been no technical trespass and even though an individual's movements in public are voluntarily exposed to third parties. As Justice Sonia Sotomayor observed in her concurring opinion, "it may be necessary to reconsider the premise that an individual has no reasonable expectation of privacy in information voluntarily disclosed to third parties... . This approach is ill- suited to the digital age, in which people reveal a great deal of information about themselves to third parties in the course of carrying out mundane tasks... . I would not assume that all information voluntarily disclosed to [others] for a limited purpose is, for that reason alone, disentitled to Fourth Amendment protection."[65]

Similarly, Justice Samuel Alito, in a concurring opinion joined by Justices Ruth Bader Ginsburg, Stephen Breyer, and Elena Kagan, declared that "'we must assur[e] preservation of that degree of privacy against government that existed when the Fourth Amendment was adopted.'"[66] Noting that modern technological advances can seriously undermine our traditional expectations of privacy, Justice Alito argued that the Fourth Amendment must take account of such changes. Although the Court in *Jones* did not overrule *Miller* and *Smith*, and left that issue for another day, a majority of the Justices clearly indicated an interest in considering how the principle recognized in those decisions should apply in a very different technological society from the one that existed in the 1970s.

However the Supreme Court ultimately resolves the Fourth Amendment issue, that question is not before us. Our charge is not to interpret the Fourth Amendment, but to make recommendations about sound public policy. In his concurring opinion in *Jones*, Justice Alito noted that "concern about new intrusions on privacy may spur the enactment of legislation to protect against these intrusions." Indeed, he added, at a time of "dramatic technological change," the "best solution to privacy concerns may be legislative," because a "legislative body is well situated to gauge changing public attitudes, to draw detailed lines, and to balance privacy and public safety in a comprehensive way."[67]

C. Section 215 and "Ordinary" Business Records

***Recommendation 1*:** We recommend that section 215 should be amended to authorize the Foreign Intelligence Surveillance Court to issue a section 215 order compelling a third party to disclose otherwise private information about particular individuals only if:

(1) it finds that the government has reasonable grounds to believe that the particular information sought is relevant to an authorized investigation intended to protect "against international terrorism or clandestine intelligence activities" and
(2) like a subpoena, the order is reasonable in focus, scope, and breadth.

As written, section 215 confers essentially subpoena-like power on the FISC, granting it the authority to order third parties to turn over to federal investigators records and other tangible objects if the government presents "a statement of facts showing that there are reasonable grounds to believe that the tangible objects sought are relevant" to an authorized investigation intended to protect "against international terrorism or clandestine intelligence activities."[68] Section 215 makes clear that, in order for records and other objects to be obtained under its authority, they must be things that "could be obtained with a subpoena issued by a court of the United States in aid of a grand jury investigation or with any other order issued by a court of the United States directing the production of records or tangible things."[69]

There are several points of comparison between the traditional subpoena and section 215: (1) section 215 deals with national security investigations rather than criminal investigations; (2) section 215 involves orders issued by the FISC, whereas subpoenas are issued in other federal district court proceedings; (3) because of the sensitive nature of national security investigations, the section 215 process involves a high degree of secrecy; and (4) section 215's "relevance" and minimization requirements effectively embody a "reasonableness" standard similar to that employed in the use of subpoenas. Assuming that the traditional subpoena is an appropriate method of gathering evidence, and that it strikes a reasonable balance between the interests of privacy and public safety in the context of criminal investigations, it might seem that, when used in a similar manner, section 215 is also an appropriate method of collecting information in the context of authorized investigations to protect "against international terrorism or clandestine intelligence activities."

We do not agree. Whereas the subpoena is typically used to obtain records pertaining to an individual or entity relevant to a particular criminal investigation, section 215 authorizes the FISC to order the production of records or other tangible objects whenever there are "reasonable grounds to believe that the tangible things sought are relevant to authorized investigations ... to protect against international terrorism or clandestine intelligence activities." The analogue in the subpoena context would be a court order directing banks and credit card companies to turn over financial information whenever *the police* conclude that they have "reasonable grounds to believe that the tangible things sought are relevant to authorized investigations" of a drug cartel.

This formulation leaves extremely broad discretion in the hands of government officials to decide for themselves *whose* records to obtain. The shift from the 1998 standard to the 2005 standard, which was adopted in the wake of the terrorist attacks of September 11, 2001, leaves too little authority in the FISC to define the appropriate parameters of section 215 orders. We believe that, as a matter of sound public policy, it is advisable for a neutral and detached judge, rather than a government investigator engaged in the "competitive enterprise" of ferreting out suspected terrorists,[70] to make the critical determination whether the government has reasonable grounds for intruding upon the legitimate privacy interests of any *particular* individual or organization. The requirement of an explicit judicial finding that the order is "reasonable in focus, scope, and breadth" is designed to ensure this critical element of judicial oversight.

D. National Security Letters

***Recommendation 2*:** We recommend that statutes that authorize the issuance of National Security Letters should be amended to permit the issuance of National Security Letters only upon a judicial finding that:

(1) the government has reasonable grounds to believe that the particular information sought is relevant to an authorized investigation intended to protect "against international terrorism or clandestine intelligence activities" and
(2) like a subpoena, the order is reasonable in focus, scope, and breadth.

***Recommendation 3*:** We recommend that all statutes authorizing the use of National Security Letters should be amended to require the use of the same oversight, minimization, retention, and dissemination standards that currently govern the use of section 215 orders.

Shortly after the decision in *Miller*, Congress created the National Security Letter (NSL) as a form of administrative subpoena.[71] NSLs, which are authorized by five separate federal statutory provisions,[72] empower the FBI and other government agencies in limited circumstances to compel individuals and organizations to turn over to the FBI in the course of national security investigations many of the same records that are covered by section 215 and that criminal prosecutors can obtain through subpoenas issued by a judge or by a prosecutor in the context of a grand jury investigation. NSLs are used primarily to obtain telephone toll records, e-mail subscriber information, and banking and credit card records. Although NSLs were initially used sparingly, the FBI issued 21,000 NSLs in Fiscal Year 2012, primarily for subscriber information. NSLs are most often used early in an investigation to gather information that might link suspected terrorists or spies to each other or to a foreign power or terrorist organization.

When NSLs were first created, the FBI was empowered to issue an NSL only if it was authorized by an official with the rank of Deputy Assistant Director or higher in the Bureau's headquarters, and only if that official certified that there were "specific and articulable facts giving reason to believe that the customer or entity whose records are sought is a foreign power or an agent of a foreign power."[73] The PATRIOT Act of 2001 significantly expanded the FBI's authority to issue NSLs. First, the PATRIOT Act authorized every Special Agent in Charge of any of the Bureau's 56 field offices around the country to issue NSLs. NSLs therefore no longer have to be issued by high-level officials at FBI headquarters.

Second, the PATRIOT Act eliminated the need for any *particularized* showing of individualized suspicion.[74] Under the PATRIOT Act, the FBI can issue an NSL whenever an authorized FBI official certifies that the records sought are "relevant to an authorized investigation." Third, the PATRIOT Act empowered the FBI to issue nondisclosure orders (sometimes referred to as "gag orders") that prohibit individuals and institutions served with NSLs from disclosing that fact, and it provided for the first time for judicial enforcement of those nondisclosure orders.[75] In contemplating the power granted to the FBI in the use of NSLs, it is important to emphasize that NSLs are issued directly by the FBI itself, rather than by a judge or by a prosecutor acting under the auspices of a grand jury.[76] Courts ordinarily enter the picture only if the recipient of an NSL affirmatively challenges its legality.[77]

NSLs have been highly controversial. This is so for several reasons. First, as already noted, NSLs are issued by FBI officials rather than by a judge or by a prosecutor in the context of a grand jury investigation. Second, as noted, the standard the FBI must meet for issuing NSLs is very low. Third, there have been serious compliance issues in the use of NSLs. In 2007, the Department of Justice's Office of the Inspector General detailed extensive misuse of the NSL authority, including the issuance of NSLs without the approval of a properly designated official and the use of NSLs in investigations for which they had not been authorized.[78] Moreover, in 2008, the Inspector General disclosed that the FBI had "issued [NSLs] ... after the FISA Court, citing First Amendment concerns, had twice declined to sign Section 215 orders in the same investigation."[79] Fourth, the oversight and minimization requirements governing the use of NSLs are much less rigorous than those imposed in the use of section 215 orders.[80] Fifth, nondisclosure orders, which are used with 97 percent of all NSLs, interfere with individual freedom and with First Amendment rights.[81]

There is one final—and important— issue about NSLs. For all the well-established reasons for requiring neutral and detached judges to decide when government investigators may invade an individual's privacy, there is a strong argument that NSLs should not be issued by the FBI itself. Although administrative subpoenas are often issued by administrative agencies, foreign intelligence investigations are especially likely to implicate highly sensitive and personal information and to have potentially severe consequences for the individuals under investigation. We are unable to identify a principled reason why NSLs should be issued by FBI officials when section 215 orders and orders for pen register and trap-and-trace surveillance must be issued by the FISC.

We recognize, however, that there are legitimate practical and logistical concerns. At the current time, a requirement that NSLs must be approved by the FISC would pose a serious logistical challenge. The FISC has only a small number of judges and the FBI currently issues an average of nearly 60 NSLs per day. It is not realistic to expect the FISC, as currently constituted, to handle that burden. This is a matter that merits further study. Several solutions may be possible, including a significant expansion in the number of FISC judges, the creation within the FISC of several federal magistrate judges to handle NSL requests, and use of the Classified Information Procedures Act[82] to enable other federal courts to issue NSLs.

We recognize that the transition to this procedure will take some time, planning, and resources, and that it would represent a significant change from the current system. We are not suggesting that the change must be undertaken immediately and without careful consideration. But it should take place as soon as reasonably possible. Once the transition is complete, NSLs should not issue without prior judicial approval, in the absence of an emergency where time is of the essence.[83] We emphasize the importance of the last point: In the face of a genuine emergency, prior judicial approval would not be required under standard and well- established principles.

E. Section 215 and the Bulk Collection of Telephony Meta-data

1. The Program

One reading of section 215 is that the phrase "reasonable grounds to believe that the tangible things sought are *relevant* to an authorized investigation" means that the order must specify with reasonable particularity the records or other things that must be turned over to the government. For example, the order might specify that a credit card company must turn over the credit records of a particular individual who is reasonably suspected of planning or participating in terrorist activities, or that a telephone company must turn over to the government the call records of any person who called an individual suspected of carrying out a terrorist act within a reasonable period of time preceding the terrorist act. This interpretation of "relevant" would be consistent with the traditional understanding of "relevance" in the subpoena context.

In May 2006, however, the FISC adopted a much broader understanding of the word "relevant."[84] It was that decision that led to the collection of bulk telephony meta-data under section 215. In that decision, and in thirty-five decisions since, fifteen different FISC judges have issued orders under section 215 directing specified United States telecommunications providers to turn over to the FBI and NSA, "on an ongoing daily basis," for a period of approximately 90 days, "all call detail records or 'telephony meta-data' created by [the provider] for communications (i) between the United States and abroad; or (ii) wholly within the United States, including local telephone calls."[85]

The "telephony meta-data" that must be produced includes "comprehensive communications routing information, including but not limited to session identifying information (e.g., originating and terminating telephone number, International Mobile Subscriber Identity (IMSI) number, International Mobile Station Equipment Identity (IMEI) number, etc.), trunk identifier, telephone calling card numbers, and time and duration of call."[86] The orders expressly provide that the meta-data to be produced "does not include the substantive content of any communication ... or the name, address, or financial information of a subscriber or customer," nor does it include "cell site location information."[87] The orders also contain a nondisclosure provision directing that, with certain exceptions, "no person shall disclose to any other person that the FBI or NSA has sought or obtained tangible things under this Order."[88]

The FISC authorized the collection of bulk telephony meta-data under section 215 in reliance "on the assertion of the [NSA] that having access to all the call records 'is vital to NSA's counterterrorism intelligence' because 'the only effective means by which NSA analysts are able continuously to keep track of'" the activities, operatives, and plans of specific foreign terrorist organizations who "disguise and obscure their communications and identities" is "'to obtain and maintain an archive of meta-data that will permit these tactics to be uncovered.'"[89] The government has explained the rationale of the program as follows:

> One of the greatest challenges the United States faces in combating international terrorism and preventing potentially catastrophic terrorist attacks on our country is identifying terrorist operatives and networks, particularly those operating within the United States. Detecting threats by exploiting terrorist communications has been, and continues to be, one of the critical tools in this effort. It is imperative that we have the capability to rapidly identify any terrorist threat inside the United States.... .

... By analyzing telephony meta-data based on telephone numbers or other identifiers associated with terrorist activity, trained expert analysts can work to determine whether known or suspected terrorists have been in contact with individuals in the United States... . In this respect, the program helps to close critical intelligence gaps that were highlighted by the September 11, 2001 attacks.[90]

What this means, in effect, is that specified service providers must turn over to the government on an ongoing basis call records for every telephone call made in, to, or from the United States through their respective systems. NSA retains the bulk telephony meta-data for a period of five years. The meta-data are then purged automatically from NSA's systems on a rolling basis. As it currently exists, the section 215 program acquires a very large amount of telephony meta-data each day, but what it collects represents only a small percentage of the total telephony meta-data held by service providers. Importantly, in 2011 NSA abandoned a similar meta-data program for Internet communications.[91]

According to the terms of the FISC orders, the following restrictions govern the use of this telephony meta-data:

1. "NSA shall storeand process the ... meta-data in repositories with secure networks under NSA's control. The ... meta-data shall carry unique markings such that software and other controls (including user authentication services) can restrict access to it to authorized personnel who have received appropriate and adequate training," and "NSA shall restrict access to the ... meta-data to authorized personnel who have received" such training.
2. "The government is ... prohibited from accessing" the meta- data "for any purpose" other than to obtain "foreign intelligence information."[92]
3. "NSA shall access the ... meta-data for purposes of obtaining foreign intelligence only through queries of the ... meta-data to obtain contact chaining information ... using selection terms approved as 'seeds' pursuant to the RAS approval process." What this means is that NSA can access the meta-data only when "there are facts giving rise to a reasonable, articulable suspicion (RAS) that the selection term to be queried," that is, the specific phone number, "is associated with" a specific foreign terrorist organization. The government submits and the FISC approves a list of specific foreign terrorist organizations to which all queries must relate.
4. The finding that there is a reasonable, articulable suspicion that any particular identifier is associated with a foreign terrorist organization can be made initially by only one of 22 specially trained persons at NSA (20 line personnel and two supervisors). All RAS determinations must be made independently by at least two of these personnel and then approved by one of the two supervisors before any query may be made.
5. Before any selection term may be queried, NSA's Office of General Counsel (OGC) "must first determine" whether it is "reasonably believed to be used by a United States person."[93] If so, then the selection term may not be queried if the OGC finds that the United States person was found be to "associated with" a specific foreign terrorist organization "solely on the basis of activities that are protected by the First Amendment to the Constitution."
6. "NSA shall ensure, through adequate and appropriate technical and management controls, that queries of the ... meta-data for intelligence analysis purposes will be

initiated using only selection terms that have been RAS-approved. Whenever the ... meta-data is accessed for foreign intelligence analysis purposes or using foreign intelligence analysis tools, an auditable record of the activity shall be generated."

7. The determination that a particular selection term may be queried remains in effect for 180 days if the selection term is reasonably believed to be used by a United States person, and otherwise for one year.
8. Before any of the results from queries may be shared outside NSA (typically with the FBI), NSA must comply with minimization and dissemination requirements, and before NSA may share any results from queries that reveal information about a United States person, a high-level official must additionally determine that the information "is in fact related to counterterrorism information and that it is necessary to understand the counterterrorism information or assess its importance."
9. The FISA court does not review or approve individual queries either in advance or after the fact. It does set the criteria for queries, however, and it receives reports every 30 days from NSA on the number of identifiers used to query the meta-data and on the results of those queries. The Department of Justice and the Senate and House Intelligence Committees also receive regular briefings on the program.
10. Both NSA and the National Security Division of the Department of Justice (NSD/DOJ) conduct regular and rigorous oversight of this program. For example:
    - NSA's OGC and Office of the Director of Compliance (ODOC) "shall ensure that personnel with access to the ... meta-data receive appropriate and adequate training and guidance regarding the procedures and restrictions for collection, storage, analysis, dissemination, and retention of the ... meta-data and the results of queries of the ... meta-data."[94]
    - NSD/DOJ receives "all formal briefing and/or training materials." NSA's ODOC "shall monitor the implementation and use of the software and other controls (including user authentication services) and the logging of auditable information."[95]
    - NSA's OGC "shall consult with NSD/DOJ "on all significant legal opinions that relate to the interpretation, scope, and/or implementation of this authority," and at least once every ninety days NSA's OGC, ODOC and NSD/DOJ "shall meet for the purpose of assessing compliance" with the FISC's orders. The results of that meeting "shall be reduced to writing and submitted" to the FISC "as part of any application to renew or reinstate the authority."[96]
    - At least once every 90 days "NSD/DOJ shall meet with NSA's Office of the Inspector General to discuss their respective oversight responsibilities and assess NSA's compliance" with the FISC's orders, and at least once every 90 days NSA's OGC and NSD/DOJ "shall review a sample of the justifications for RAS approvals for selection terms used to query the ... meta-data."[97]
    - Approximately every 30 days, NSA must file with the FISC "a report that includes a discussion of NSA's application of the RAS standard," "a statement of the number of instances ... in which NSA has shared, in any form, results from queries of the ... meta-data that contain United States person information, in any form, with anyone outside NSA," and an attestation for each instance in which United States information has been shared that "the information was related to

counterterrorism information and necessary to understand counterterrorism or to assess its importance."[98]

How does the section 215 bulk telephony meta-data program work in practice? In 2012, NSA queried 288 unique identifiers, each of which was certified by NSA analysts to meet the RAS standard. When an identifier, or "seed" phone number, is queried, NSA receives a list of every telephone number that either called or was called by the seed phone number in the past five years. This is known as the "first hop." For example, if the seed phone number was in contact with 100 different phone numbers in the past five years, NSA would have a list of those phone numbers. Given that NSA has reasonable articulable suspicion to believe that the seed phone number is associated with a foreign terrorist organization, it then seeks to determine whether there is any reason to believe that any of the 100 numbers are *also* associated with a foreign terrorist organization. If so, the query has uncovered possible connections to a potential terrorist network that merits further investigation. Conversely, if none of the 100 numbers in the above hypothetical is believed to be associated with possible terrorist activity, there is less reason to be concerned that the potential terrorist is in contact with co-conspirators in the United States.

In most cases, NSA makes a second "hop." That is, it queries the database to obtain a list of every phone number that called or was called by the 100 numbers it obtained in the first hop. To continue with the hypothetical: If we assume that the average telephone number called or was called by 100 phone numbers over the course of the five-year period, the query will produce a list of 10,000 phone numbers (100 x 100) that are two "hops" away from the person reasonably believed to be associated with a foreign terrorist organization. If one of those 10,000 phone numbers is thought to be associated with a terrorist organization, that is potentially useful information not only with respect to the individuals related to the first and third hops, but also with respect to individuals related to the second hop (the middleman). In a very few instances, NSA makes a third "hop," which would expand the list of numbers to approximately one million (100 x 100 x 100).

In 2012, NSA's 288 queries resulted in a total of twelve "tips" to the FBI that called for further investigation. If the FBI investigates a telephone number or other identifier tipped to it through the section 215 program, it must rely on other information to identify the individual subscribers of any of the numbers retrieved. If, through further investigation, the FBI is able to develop probable cause to believe that an identifier in the United States is conspiring with a person engaged in terrorist activity, it can then seek an order from the FISC authorizing it to intercept the *contents* of future communications to and from that telephone number.

NSA believes that on at least a few occasions, information derived from the section 215 bulk telephony meta-data program has contributed to its efforts to prevent possible terrorist attacks, either in the United States or somewhere else in the world. More often, negative results from section 215 queries have helped to alleviate concern that particular terrorist suspects are in contact with co-conspirators in the United States. Our review suggests that the information contributed to terrorist investigations by the use of section 215 telephony meta-data was not essential to preventing attacks and could readily have been obtained in a timely manner using conventional section 215 orders. Moreover, there is reason for caution about the view that the program is efficacious in alleviating concern about possible terrorist connections, given the fact that the meta-data captured by the program covers only a portion of the records of only a few telephone service providers.

The bulk telephony meta-data collection program has experienced several significant compliance issues. For example, in March 2009, the FISC learned that for two-and-a-half years NSA had searched all incoming phone meta-data using an "alert list" of phone numbers of possible terrorists that had been created for other purposes. Almost 90 percent of the numbers on the alert list did *not* meet the "reasonable, articulable suspicion" standard.[99]

FISC Judge Reggie Walton concluded that the minimization procedures had been "so frequently and systematically violated that it can fairly be said that this critical element of the overall ... regime has never functioned effectively."[100] Although finding that the noncompliance was unintentional, and was due to misunderstandings on the part of analysts about the precise rules governing their use of the meta-data, Judge Walton concluded "that the government's failure to ensure that responsible officials adequately understood NSA's alert list process, and to accurately report its implementation to the Court, has prevented, for more than two years, both the government and the FISC from taking steps to remedy daily violations of the minimization procedures set forth in FISC orders and designed to protect ... call details pertaining to telephone communications of US persons located within the United States who are not the subject of any ... investigation and whose call detail information could not otherwise have been legally captured in bulk."[101]

Judge Walton found additional compliance issues involving incidents in which inadequately trained analysts "had queried the ... meta-data ... 'without being aware they were doing so.'"[102] As a result, "NSA analysts used 2,373 foreign telephone identifiers to query the ... meta-data without first determining that the reasonable, articulable suspicion standard had been satisfied." Judge Walton concluded that "the minimization procedures" that had been "approved and adopted as binding by the orders of the FISC have been so frequently and systematically violated that it can fairly be said that this critical element of the overall [bulk telephony meta-data] regime has never functioned effectively."[103]

Although NSA maintained that, upon learning of these noncompliance incidents, it had taken remedial measures to prevent them from recurring, Judge Walton rejected the government's argument that, in light of these measures, "the Court need not take any further remedial action." Because it had become apparent that "NSA's data accessing technologies and practices were never adequately designed to comply with the governing minimization procedures," NSA Director General Keith Alexander conceded that "there was no single person who had a complete understanding of the [section 215] FISA system architecture."[104]

In light of that concession and other information, Judge Walton held that "the Court will not permit the government to access the data collected until such time as the government is able to restore the Court's confidence that the government can and will comply with [the] approved procedures for accessing such data." Until such time, the government would be permitted to access the data only subject to a FISC order authorizing a specific query "on a case-by-case" basis premised on a RAS finding by the FISC itself.[105]

Judge Walton lifted this restriction in September 2009 after NSA demonstrated to his satisfaction that the causes of the noncompliance had been corrected and that additional safeguards had been instituted to reduce the possibility of similar incidents of noncompliance in the future.[106]

It is noteworthy that, after the bulk telephony meta-data program came to light in the summer of 2013, some commentators argued that the program is both unconstitutional and beyond the scope of what Congress authorized. The constitutional argument turns largely on whether *Miller* and *Smith* are still good law and on whether they should control the collection of bulk telephony meta-data. In a recent FISC opinion, Judge Mary A. McLaughlin acknowledged that the "Supreme Court may someday revisit the third-party disclosure principle in the context of twenty-first century communications technology," but concluded that until that day arrives, "*Smith* remains controlling with respect to the acquisition by the government from service providers of non-content telephony meta- data."[107]

The statutory objection asserts that the FISC's interpretation of section 215 does violence to the word "relevant." Some commentators have noted that, although courts have upheld relatively broad subpoenas in the context of civil actions, administrative proceedings and grand jury investigations, "no single subpoena discussed in a reported decision is as broad as the FISC's telephony meta-data orders."[108] Nonetheless, in a recent FISC decision, Judge Claire V. Eagen concluded that the bulk telephony meta-data program meets what she described as "the low statutory hurdle set out in Section 215."[109] Our charge is not to resolve these questions, but to offer guidance from the perspective of sound public policy as we look to the future.

2. The Mass Collection of Personal Information

***Recommendation 4*:** We recommend that, as a general rule, and without senior policy review, the government should not be permitted to collect and store all mass, undigested, non-public personal information about individuals to enable future queries and data-mining for foreign intelligence purposes. Any program involving government collection or storage of such data must be narrowly tailored to serve an important government interest.

We will turn shortly to the section 215 bulk telephony meta-data program. But to orient that discussion and to establish governing principles, we begin with a broader question, which involves the production not only of telephone calling records, but also of every other type of record or other tangible thing that could be obtained through a traditional subpoena, including bank records, credit card records, medical records, travel records, Internet search records, e-mail records, educational records, library records, and so on.

Our focus, then, is on genuinely mass collections of all undigested, non-public personal information about individuals – those collections that involve not a selected or targeted subset (such as airline passenger lists), but far broader collections. Although the government has expressly disclaimed any interest in such mass collection of personal information under section 215,[110] nothing in the statute, as interpreted by the FISC, would necessarily preclude such a program. The question is whether such a program, even if consistent with the Fourth Amendment and section 215, would be sound public policy.

Because international terrorists inevitably leave footprints when they recruit, train, finance, and plan their operations, government acquisition and analysis of such personal information might provide useful clues about their transactions, movements, behavior, identities and plans. It might, in other words, help the government find the proverbial needles in the haystack. But because such information overwhelmingly concerns the behavior of ordinary, law-abiding individuals, there is a substantial risk of serious invasions of privacy.

As a report of the National Academy of Sciences (NAS) has observed, the mass collection of such personal information by the government would raise serious "concerns about the misuse and abuse of data, about the accuracy of the data and the manner in which the data are aggregated, and about the possibility that the government could, through its collection and analysis of data, inappropriately influence individuals' conduct."[111] According to the NAS report, "data and communication streams" are ubiquitous:

> [They] concern financial transactions, medical records, travel, communications, legal proceedings, consumer preferences, Web searches, and, increasingly, behavior and biological information. This is the essence of the information age—... everyone leaves personal digital tracks in these systems whenever he or she makes a purchase, takes a trip, uses a bank account, makes a phone call, walks past a security camera, obtains a prescription, sends or receives a package, files income tax forms, applies for a loan, e-mails a friend, sends a fax, rents a video, or engages in just about any other activity ... . Gathering and analyzing [such data] can play major roles in the prevention, detection, and mitigation of terrorist attacks... . [But even] under the pressures of threats as serious as terrorism, the privacy rights and civil liberties that are cherished core values of our nation must not be destroyed... .
>
> One ... concern is that law-abiding citizens who come to believe that their behavior is watched too closely by government agencies ... may be unduly inhibited from participating in the democratic process, may be inhibited from contributing fully to the social and cultural life of their communities, and may even alter their purely private and perfectly legal behavior for fear that discovery of intimate details of their lives will be revealed and used against them in some manner.[112]

Despite these concerns, several arguments can be made in support of allowing the government to collect and access *all* of this information. First, one might argue, building on the logic of *Miller* and *Smith*, that individuals are not concerned about the privacy of such matters because, if they were, they would not voluntarily make the information available to their banks, credit card companies, Internet service providers, telephone companies, health-care providers, and so on.

Whatever the logic of this argument in the Fourth Amendment context, it seems both unrealistic and unsound as a matter of public policy. In modern society, individuals, for practical reasons, have to use banks, credit cards, e-mail, telephones, the Internet, medical services, and the like. Their decision to reveal otherwise private information to such third parties does not reflect a lack of concern for the privacy of the information, but a necessary accommodation to the realities of modern life. What they want— and reasonably expect—is *both* the ability to use such services *and* the right to maintain their privacy when they do so. As a matter of sound public policy in a free society, there is no reason why that should not be possible.

Second, one might argue that there is nothing to fear from such a program because the government will query the information database only when it has good reasons for doing so. Assume, for example, that the government has legal authority to query the hypothetical mass information database only when it can demonstrate facts that give rise to a reasonable, articulable suspicion that the target of the query is associated with a foreign terrorist organization. That restriction certainly reduces the concern about widespread invasions of privacy because it would deny the government legal authority to query the database to obtain private information about individuals for other, less worthy—and perhaps illegitimate—reasons.

But this does not eliminate the concern. For one thing, under any such standard there will inevitably be many queries of individuals who are not in fact involved with terrorist organizations. This is the false positive— or inadvertent acquisition—problem. Whenever the government investigates individuals on grounds less demanding than absolute certainty of guilt, there will inevitably be false positives. Even when the government has a warrant based on a judicial finding of probable cause, innocent persons will often be searched because probable cause is a far cry from absolute certainty.

One way to mitigate this concern would be to elevate the standard for lawful queries under section 215 from reasonable articulable suspicion to probable cause. But even that would leave privacy at risk. This is so because, in traditional searches, the government does not discover *everything* there is to know about an individual. The enormity of the breach of privacy caused by queries of the hypothetical mass information database dwarfs the privacy invasion occasioned by more traditional forms of investigation. For the innocent individual who is unlucky enough to be queried under even a probable cause standard, virtually *everything* about his life instantly falls into the hands of government officials. The most intimate details of his life are laid bare.

Moreover, and perhaps more important, there is the lurking danger of abuse. There is always a risk that the rules, however reasonable in theory, will not be followed in practice. This might happen because an analyst with access to the information decides to query an innocent individual for any number of possible reasons, ranging from personal animosity to blackmail to political opposition. Although the safeguards in place under section 215 attempt to prevent such abuse, no system is perfect. We have seen that even under section 215, with all of its safeguards, there have been serious issues of noncompliance. A breach of privacy might also happen because an outsider manages to invade the database, thereby accessing and then either using or publicly disclosing reams of information about particular individuals or, in the nightmare scenario, making the entire system transparent to *everyone*.

Finally, we cannot discount the risk, in light of the lessons of our own history, that at some point in the future, high-level government officials will decide that this massive database of extraordinarily sensitive private information is there for the plucking. Americans must never make the mistake of wholly "trusting" our public officials. As the Church Committee observed more than 35 years ago, when the capacity of government to collect massive amounts of data about individual Americans was still in its infancy, the "massive centralization of ... information creates a temptation to use it for improper purposes, threatens to 'chill' the exercise of First Amendment rights, and is inimical to the privacy of citizens."[113]

Third, one might argue that, despite these concerns, the hypothetical mass collection of personal information would make it easier for the government to protect the nation from terrorism, and it should therefore be permitted. We take this argument seriously. But even if the premise is true, the conclusion does not necessarily follow. Every limitation on the government's ability to monitor our conduct makes it more difficult for the government to prevent bad things from happening. As our risk- management principle suggests, the question is not whether granting the government authority makes us incrementally safer, but whether the additional safety is worth the sacrifice in terms of individual privacy, personal liberty, and public trust.

Although we might be safer if the government had ready access to a massive storehouse of information about every detail of our lives, the impact of such a program on the quality of life and on individual freedom would simply be too great. And this is especially true in light of the alternative measures available to the government. Specifically, even if the government cannot collect and store for future use massive amounts of personal information about our lives, it would still be free under section 215 to obtain *specific* information relating to *specific* individuals or *specific* terrorist threats from banks, telephone companies, credit card companies, and the like—when it can demonstrate to the FISC that it has *reasonable grounds* to access such information.

3. Is Meta-Data Different?

***Recommendation 5*:** We recommend that legislation should be enacted that terminates the storage of bulk telephony meta-data by the government under section 215, and transitions as soon as reasonably possible to a system in which such meta-data is held instead either by private providers or by a private third party. Access to such data should be permitted only with a section 215 order from the Foreign Intelligence Surveillance Court that meets the requirements set forth in Recommendation 1.

Under section 215 as interpreted by the FISC, NSA is authorized to collect bulk telephony meta-data and to store the call records of *every* telephone call made in, to, or from the United States, and it is then permitted to query that meta-data if it has a reasonable, articulable suspicion that a particular phone number, or "seed," usually a telephone number belonging to a person outside the United States, is associated with a foreign terrorist organization. Section 215 as interpreted authorizes the collection and retention only of *telephony* meta-data. Should that limitation make the program permissible?

We do not believe so. There are two distinctions between the hypothetical and actual versions of section 215. First, the total amount of data collected and retained in the hypothetical version of section 215 is *much* greater than the total amount of data collected and retained in the actual version. This means that the possible harm caused by the collection and the possible benefit derived from the collection are *both* reduced. Everything else being equal, this suggests that the balance between costs and benefits is unchanged.[114]

Second, and more important, it is often argued that the collection of bulk telephony meta-data does not seriously threaten individual privacy, because it involves only transactional information rather than the content of the communications. Indeed, this is a central argument in defense of the existing program. It does seem reasonable to assume that the intrusion on privacy is greater if the government collects the content of every telephone call made in, to, or from the United States than if it collects only the call information, or meta-data. But as critics of the bulk collection of telephony meta-data have observed, the record of every telephone call an individual makes or receives over the course of several years can reveal an enormous amount about that individual's private life.

We do not mean to overstate either the problem or the risks. In our review, we have not uncovered any official efforts to suppress dissent or any intent to intrude into people's private lives without legal justification. NSA is interested in protecting the national security, not in personal details unrelated to that concern. But as as Justice Sotomayor observed about GPS monitoring of locational information in *Jones*, telephone calling data can reveal "a wealth of detail" about an individual's "familial, political, professional, religious, and sexual associations."[115] It can reveal calls "to the psychiatrist, the plastic surgeon, the abortion clinic, the AIDS treatment center, the strip club, the criminal defense attorney, the by-the-hour-motel, the union meeting, the mosque, synagogue or church, the gay bar, and on and on."[116]

Knowing that the government has ready access to one's phone call records can seriously chill "associational and expressive freedoms," and knowing that the government is one flick of a switch away from such information can profoundly "alter the relationship between citizen and government in a way that is inimical to society."[117] That knowledge can significantly undermine public trust, which is exceedingly important to the well-being of a free and open society.

Moreover, and importantly, even without collecting and storing bulk telephony meta-data itself, there are alternative ways for the government to achieve its legitimate goals, while significantly limiting the invasion of privacy and the risk of government abuse. As originally envisioned when section 215 was enacted, the government can query the information directly from the relevant service providers after obtaining an order from the FISC. Although this process might be less efficient for the government, NSA Director General Keith Alexander informed the Review Group that NSA itself has seriously considered moving to a model in which the data are held by the private sector. This change would greatly reduce the intake of telephony meta-data by NSA, and it would therefore also dramatically (and in our view appropriately) reduce the risk, both actual and perceived, of government abuse.

We recognize that there might be problems in querying multiple, privately held data bases simultaneously and expeditiously. In our view, however, it is likely that those problems can be significantly reduced by creative engineering approaches. We also recognize that there might be issues about the length of time that some carriers ordinarily would retain such meta-data and about the financial costs that might be placed on telephony providers by the approach we recommend. But we think that it would be in the interests of the providers and the government to agree on a voluntary system that meets the needs of both. If a voluntary approach is not successful, then implementing legislation might be required.[118]

If reliance on government queries to individual service providers proves to be so inefficient that it seriously undermines the effectiveness of the program, and if the program is shown to be of substantial value to our capacity to protect the national security of the United States and our allies, then the government might authorize a specially designated private organization to collect and store the bulk telephony meta-data. NSA could then query the meta-data from that independent entity in the same manner that it could query the meta-data from the service providers. The use of such a private organization to collect and store bulk telephony meta-data should be implemented only if expressly authorized by Congress.

In light of these alternatives, we conclude that there is no sufficient justification for allowing the government itself to collect and store bulk telephony meta-data.[119] We recommend that this program should be terminated as soon as reasonably practicable.

***Recommendation 6*:** We recommend that the government should commission a study of the legal and policy options for assessing the distinction between meta- data and other types of information. The study should include technological experts and persons with a diverse range of perspectives, including experts about the missions of intelligence and law enforcement agencies and about privacy and civil liberties.

Are there any circumstances in which the government should be permitted to collect and retain meta-data in which it could not collect and retain other information? One question concerns the meaning of "meta- data." In the telephony context, "meta-data" refers to technical information about the phone numbers, routing information, duration of the call, time of the call, and so forth. It does not include information about the contents of the call. In the e-mail context, "meta-data" refers to the "to" and "from" lines in the e-mail and technical details about the e-mail, but not the subject line or the content. The assumption behind the argument that meta-data is meaningfully different from other information is that the collection of meta-data does not seriously invade individual privacy.

As we have seen, however, that assumption is questionable. In a world of ever more complex technology, it is increasingly unclear whether the distinction between "meta-data" and other information carries much weight.[120] The quantity and variety of meta-data have increased. In contrast to the telephone call records at issue in the 1979 case of *Smith v. Maryland*,[121] today's mobile phone calls create meta-data about a person's location. Social networks provide constant updates about who is communicating with whom, and that information is considered meta-data rather than content. E-mails, texts, voice-over-IP calls, and other forms of electronic communication have multiplied. For Internet communications in general, the shift to the IPv6 protocol is well under way. When complete, web communications will include roughly 200 data fields, in addition to the underlying content. Although the legal system has been slow to catch up with these major changes in meta-data, it may well be that, as a practical matter, the distinction itself should be discarded.

The question about how to govern content and meta-data merits further study. Such a study should draw on the insights of technologists, due to the central role of changing technology. Economists and other social scientists should help assess the costs and benefits of alternative approaches. The study should include diverse persons, with a range of perspectives about the mission of intelligence and law enforcement agencies and also with expertise with respect to privacy and civil liberties.

F. Secrecy and Transparency

***Recommendation 7*:** We recommend that legislation should be enacted requiring that detailed information about authorities such as those involving National Security Letters, section 215 business records, section 702, pen register and trap-and-trace, and the section 215 bulk telephony meta-data program should be made available on a regular basis to Congress and the American people to the greatest extent possible, consistent with the need to protect classified information. With respect to authorities and programs whose existence is unclassified, there should be a strong presumption of transparency to enable the American people and their elected representatives independently to assess the merits of the programs for themselves.

***Recommendation 8*:** We recommend that:

(1) legislation should be enacted providing that, in the use of National Security Letters, section 215 orders, pen register and trap-and-trace orders, 702 orders, and similar orders directing individuals, businesses, or other institutions to turn over information to the government, non-disclosure orders may be issued only upon a judicial finding that there are reasonable grounds to believe that disclosure would significantly threaten the national security, interfere with an ongoing investigation, endanger the life or physical safety of any person, impair diplomatic relations, or put at risk some other similarly weighty government or foreign intelligence interest;
(2) nondisclosure orders should remain in effect for no longer than 180 days without judicial re-approval; and
(3) nondisclosure orders should never be issued in a manner that prevents the recipient of the order from seeking legal counsel in order to challenge the order's legality.

***Recommendation 9*:** We recommend that legislation should be enacted providing that, even when nondisclosure orders are appropriate, recipients of National Security Letters, section 215 orders, pen register and trap-and-trace orders, section 702 orders, and similar orders issued in programs whose existence is unclassified may publicly disclose on a periodic basis general information about the number of such orders they have received, the number they have complied with, the general categories of information they have produced, and the number of users whose information they have produced in each category, unless the government makes a compelling demonstration that such disclosures would endanger the national security.

***Recommendation 10*:** We recommend that, building on current law, the government should publicly disclose on a regular basis general data about National Security Letters, section 215 orders, pen register and trap-and-trace orders, section 702 orders, and similar orders in programs whose existence is unclassified, unless the government makes a compelling demonstration that such disclosures would endanger the national security.

***Recommendation 11*:** We recommend that the decision to keep secret from the American people programs of the magnitude of the section 215 bulk telephony meta-data program should be made only after careful deliberation at high levels of government and only with due consideration of and respect for the strong presumption of transparency that is central to democratic governance. A program of this magnitude should be kept secret from the American people only if (a) the program serves a compelling governmental interest and (b) the efficacy of the program would be *substantially* impaired if our enemies were to know of its existence.

A free people can govern themselves only if they have access to the information that they need to make wise judgments about public policy. A government that unnecessarily shields its policies and decisions from public scrutiny therefore undermines the most central premise of a free and self-governing society. As James Madison observed, "A popular Government, without popular information, or the means of acquiring it, is but a Prologue to a Farce or a Tragedy; or, perhaps both."[122]

There is no doubt that in the realm of national security, the nation needs to keep secrets. The question, though, is what information must be kept secret. The reasons why government officials want secrecy are many and varied. They range from the truly compelling to the patently illegitimate. Sometimes government officials want secrecy because they rightly fear that the disclosure of certain information might seriously undermine the nation's security. Sometimes they want secrecy because they do not want to have to deal with public criticism of their decisions or because they do not want the public, Congress, or the courts to override their decisions, which they believe to be wise. Sometimes they want secrecy because disclosure will expose their own incompetence, noncompliance, or wrongdoing. Some of those reasons for secrecy are obviously more worthy of deference than others.

Adding to the complexity, the contribution of any particular disclosure to informed public discourse may vary widely depending upon the nature of the information. The disclosure of some confidential information may be extremely valuable to public debate (for example, the revelation of unwise or even unlawful government programs). The disclosure of other confidential information, however, may be of little or no legitimate value to public debate (for example, publication of the identities of covert American agents). The most vexing problems arise when the public disclosure of secret information is *both* harmful to national security *and* valuable to informed self-governance.

There is a compelling need today for a serious and comprehensive reexamination of the balance between secrecy and transparency. In considering this question, the Public Interest Declassification Board (PIDB) recently observed: "A Democratic society is grounded in the informed participation of the citizenry, and their informed participation requires access to Government information. An open record of official decisions is essential to educate and inform the public and enable it to assess the policies of its elected leaders. If officials are to be accountable for their actions and decisions, secrecy must be kept to the minimum required to meet legitimate national security considerations... . Better access to Government records and internal history will help both policymakers and the American public meet their mutual responsibilities to address national security and foreign policy challenges consistent with democratic values." The PIDB concluded that it is necessary for the United States to make the reforms necessary "to transform current classification and declassification guidance and practice."[123]

Another dimension to the secrecy vs. transparency issue concerns the role of whistle-blowers. Although an individual government employee or contractor should not take it upon himself to decide on his own to "leak" classified information because he thinks it would be better for the nation for the information to be disclosed, it is also the case that a free and democratic nation needs safe, reliable, and fair-minded processes to enable such individuals to present their concerns to responsible and independent officials. After all, their concerns might be justified. It does not serve the nation for our government to prevent information that should be disclosed from being disclosed. Although such mechanisms exist, they can certainly be strengthened and made more accessible.[124] Appendix D sets forth existing mechanisms for whistle-blowing.

The secrecy vs. transparency issue also has serious repercussions today for the freedom of the press. It is the responsibility of our free press to expose abuse, over-reaching, waste, undue influence, corruption, and bad judgment on the part of our elected officials. A robust and fearless freedom of the press is essential to a flourishing self-governing society. It will not do for the press to be fearful, intimidated, or cowed by government officials. If they are, it is "We the People" who will suffer. Part of the responsibility of our free press is to ferret out and expose information that government officials would prefer to keep secret when such secrecy is unwarranted. This point raises fundamental issues about press shield laws, spying on members of the press and their sources, investigating members of the press, and attempting to intimidate members of the press.

At the same time, the potential danger of leaks is more serious than ever, especially in light of the fact that information can be spread instantly across the globe. The fact that classified information can now be stolen, either by insiders or outsiders, in massive quantities, creates unprecedented dangers. Put simply, the stakes on both sides—national security and effective self-governance—are high.

At the very least, we should always be prepared to question claims that secrecy is necessary. That conclusion needs to be demonstrated rather than merely assumed. When it is possible to promote transparency without appreciably sacrificing important competing interests, we should err on the side of transparency.

Thus, in implementing NSLs, section 215 orders, pen register and trap-and-trace orders, section 702 orders, and similar orders in programs whose existence is unclassified, the government should, to the greatest extent possible, report publicly on the total number of requests made and the number of individuals whose records have been requested. These totals inform Congress and the public about the overall size and trends in a program, and are especially informative when there are major changes in the scale of a program. In addition, providers have shown a strong interest in providing periodic transparency reports about the number of requests to which they have responded. Reports from providers can be a useful supplement to reports from the government—the existence of multiple sources of information reduces the risk of inaccurate reporting by any one source. Reports from providers are also an important way for providers to assure customers and the general public that they are careful stewards of their users' records. As discussed in Section VII, such transparency reports from providers should be permitted and encouraged by governments throughout the world, and the US Government should work with allies to enable accurate reporting about government requests in other countries as well as in the United States.

In some instances, over-reporting can also be a problem. This might occur when there are duplicative reports, which burden agencies with redundant requirements. To address this concern, the government should catalog the current reporting requirements on FISA, NSLs, and other intelligence-related statistics, and document how frequently these reports are made and to whom. As shown in Appendix C, multiple oversight mechanisms exist for reporting to Congress and within the Executive Branch. A catalog of existing reports would create a more informed basis for deciding what changes in reporting might be appropriate. Moreover, in some instances public reports can unintentionally harm the national security by inadvertently revealing critical information. For instance, detailed reports by small Internet service providers about government requests for information might inadvertently tip off terrorists or others who are properly under surveillance. To reduce this risk, reporting requirements should be less detailed in those situations in which reporting about a small number events might reveal critical information to those under surveillance.[125]

SECTION IV. REFORMING FOREIGN INTELLIGENCE SURVEILLANCE DIRECTED AT NON-UNITED STATES PERSONS

A. Introduction

To what extent should the United States accord non-United States persons the same privacy protections it recognizes for United States persons? At one level, it is easy to say that "all persons are created equal" and that every nation should accord all persons the same rights, privileges and immunities that it grants to its own citizens. But, of course, no nation follows such a policy. Nations see themselves as distinct communities with particular obligations to the members of their own community. On the other hand, there are certain fundamental rights and liberties that all nations should accord to all persons, such as the international prohibition on torture.

In this section, we explore the non-United States person issue in the specific content of foreign intelligence surveillance. International law recognizes the right of privacy as fundamental,[126] but the concrete meaning of that right must be defined. Certainly, a nation can choose to grant its own citizens a greater degree of privacy than international law requires.

We focus specifically on foreign intelligence collection under section 702 of FISA and Executive Order 12333. The central question we address is: What is the *minimum* degree of privacy protection the United States should grant to non-United States persons in the realm of foreign intelligence surveillance? We conclude that the United States should grant greater privacy protection to non-United States persons than we do today.

B. Foreign Intelligence Surveillance and Section 702

In general, the federal government is prohibited from intercepting the contents of private telephone calls and e-mails of *any* person, except in three circumstances. First, in the context of criminal investigations, Title III of the Electronic Communications Privacy Act authorizes the government to intercept such communications if a federal judge issues a warrant based on a finding that there is probable cause to believe that an individual is committing, has committed, or is about to commit a federal crime and that communications concerning that crime will be seized as a result of the proposed interception.[127]

Second, as enacted in 1978, FISA authorized the federal government to intercept electronic communications if a judge of the FISC issues a warrant based on a finding that the purpose of the surveillance is to obtain *foreign intelligence information*, the interception takes place *inside the United States*, and there is probable cause to believe that the target of the surveillance is an agent of a foreign power (which includes, among other things, individuals engaged in international terrorism, the international proliferation of weapons of mass destruction, and clandestine intelligence activities).

Third, there is foreign intelligence surveillance that takes place *outside the United States*. At the time FISA was enacted, Congress expressly decided not to address the issue of electronic surveillance of persons located outside the United States, including American citizens, noting that the "standards and procedures for overseas surveillance may have to be different than those provided in this bill for electronic surveillance within the United States."[128] It was apparently assumed that intelligence collection activities outside the United States would be conducted under the Executive Branch's inherent constitutional authority and the statutory authorizations granted to each Intelligence Community agency by Congress, and that it would be governed by presidential Executive Orders and by procedures approved by the Attorney General. To that end, in 1981 President Ronald Reagan issued Executive Order 12333, discussed above, which (as amended) specifies the circumstances in which the nation's intelligence agencies can engage in foreign intelligence surveillance outside the United States.[129]

Although Congress did not take up this issue in the immediate aftermath of the terrorist attacks of September 11, 2001, several developments brought the question to the fore. First, technological advances between 1978 and the early 21st century complicated the implementation of the original FISA rules. The distinction FISA drew between electronic surveillance conducted inside the United States and electronic surveillance conducted outside the United States worked reasonably well in 1978, because then-existing methods of communication and collection made that distinction meaningful. But the development of a global Internet communications grid with linchpins located within the United States undermined the distinction.

By the early twenty-first century, a large percentage of the world's electronic communications passed through the United States, and foreign intelligence collection against persons located outside the United States was therefore increasingly conducted with the assistance of service providers inside the United States. Unless the legislation was amended, this new state of affairs meant that the government would have to go to the FISC to obtain orders authorizing electronic surveillance for foreign intelligence purposes even of individuals who were in fact *outside* the United States, a state of affairs Congress had not anticipated at the time it enacted FISA in 1978.

Second, in late 2005 it came to light that, shortly after the attacks of September 11, President George W. Bush had secretly authorized NSA to conduct foreign intelligence surveillance of individuals who were *inside* the United States without complying with FISA. Specifically, the President authorized NSA to monitor electronic communications (e.g., telephone calls and e-mails) between people inside the United States and people outside the United States whenever NSA had "a reasonable basis to conclude that one party to the communication" was affiliated with or working in support of al-Qa'ida.

Because this secret program did not require the government either to obtain a warrant from the FISC or to demonstrate that it had probable cause that the target of the surveillance was an agent of a foreign power— even when the target was inside the United States—it clearly exceeded the bounds of what Congress had authorized in FISA. The Bush administration maintained that this program was nonetheless lawful, invoking both Congress' 2001 Authorization to Use Military Force and the President's inherent constitutional authority as commander-in-chief.

In light of these developments, Congress decided to revisit FISA. In 2007, Congress amended FISA in the Protect America Act (PAA), which provided, among other things, that FISA was inapplicable to any electronic surveillance that was "directed at a person reasonably believed to be located outside the United States."[130] In effect, the PAA excluded from the protections of FISA warrantless monitoring of international communications if the target of the surveillance was outside the United States, even if the target was an American citizen. The PAA was sharply criticized on the ground that it gave the government too much authority to target the international communications of American citizens.

The following year, Congress revised the law again in the FISA Amendments Act of 2008 (FAA). The FAA adopted different rules for international communications depending on whether the target of the surveillance was a "*United States person*" (a category that was defined to include both American citizens and non-citizens who are legal permanent residents of the United States)[131] or a "*non-United States person.*"[132] The FAA provides that if the government targets a United States person who is outside the United States, the surveillance must satisfy the traditional requirements of FISA. That is, the surveillance is permissible only if it is intended to acquire foreign intelligence information and the FISC issues a warrant based on a finding that there is probable cause to believe that the United States person is an agent of a foreign power, within the meaning of FISA. Thus, if the target of the surveillance is a United States person, the same FISA procedures apply—without regard to whether the target is inside or outside the United States.

On the other hand, the FAA provided in section 702 that if the target of foreign intelligence surveillance is a *non-United States person* who is "reasonably believed to be located outside the United States," the government need not have probable cause to believe that the target is an agent of a foreign power and need not obtain an individual warrant from the FISC, even if the interception takes place *inside* the United States. Rather, section 702 authorized the FISC to approve annual certifications submitted by the Attorney General and the Director of National Intelligence (DNI) that identify certain *categories* of foreign intelligence targets whose communications may be collected, subject to FISC-approved targeting and minimization procedures. The categories of targets specified by these certifications typically consist of, for example, international terrorists and individuals involved in the proliferation of weapons of mass destruction.

Under section 702, the determination of which *individuals* to target pursuant to these FISC-approved certifications is made by NSA without any additional FISC approval. In implementing this authority, NSA identifies specific "identifiers" (for example, e-mail addresses or telephone numbers) that it reasonably believes are being used by non-United States persons located outside of the United States to communicate foreign intelligence information within the scope of the approved categories (*e.g.*, international terrorism, nuclear proliferation, and hostile cyber activities). NSA then acquires the content of telephone calls, e-mails, text messages, photographs, and other Internet traffic using those identifiers from service providers in the United States.[133]

Illustrative identifiers might be an e-mail account used by a suspected terrorist abroad or other means used by by high-level terrorist leaders in two separate countries to pass messages. The number of identifiers for which NSA collects information under section 702 has gradually increased over time.

Section 702 requires that NSA's certifications attest that a "significant purpose" of any acquisition is to obtain foreign intelligence information (i.e. directed at international terrorism, nuclear proliferation, or hostile cyber activities), that it does not intentionally target a United States person, that it does not intentionally target any person known at the time of acquisition to be in the United States, that it does not target any person outside the United States for the purpose of targeting a person inside the United States, and that it meets the requirements of the Fourth Amendment.[134] The annual certification provided to the FISC must attest that the Attorney General and the Director of National Intelligence have adopted guidelines to ensure compliance with these and other requirements under section 702, including that the government does not intentionally use section 702 authority to target United States persons, inside or outside the United States.[135] The FISC annually reviews the targeting and minimization procedures to ensure that they satisfy all statutory and constitutional requirements.

Other significant restrictions govern the use of section 702:

- If a section 702 acquisition inadvertently obtains a communication of or concerning a United States person, section 702's minimization procedures require that any information about such a United States person must be destroyed unless there are compelling reasons to retain it, for example, if the information reveals a communications security vulnerability or an imminent threat of serious harm to life or property.
- If a target reasonably believed to be a non-United States person located outside the United States either enters the United States or is discovered to be a United States person, acquisition must immediately be terminated.

- Any information collected after a non-United States person target enters the United States must promptly be destroyed, unless it constitutes evidence of criminal conduct or has significant foreign intelligence value.
- Any information collected prior to the discovery that a target believed to be a non-United States person is in fact a United States person must be promptly destroyed, unless it constitutes evidence of criminal conduct or has significant foreign intelligence value.
- The dissemination of any information about a United States person collected during the course of a section 702 acquisition is prohibited, unless it is necessary to understand foreign intelligence or assess its importance, is evidence of criminal conduct, or indicates an imminent threat of death or serious bodily injury.

Section 702 imposes substantial reporting requirements on the government in order to enable both judicial and congressional oversight, in addition to the oversight conducted within the Executive Branch by the Department of Justice (DOJ), the Office of the Director of National Intelligence (ODNI), and the Inspectors Generals of the various agencies that make up the Intelligence Community:

- Approximately every 15 days, a team of attorneys from the National Security Division (NSD) of the DOJ and ODNI reviews the documentation underlying every new identifier tasked by NSA for collection. The team makes two judgments about each identifier: (1) Is the target a non-United States person reasonably believed to be located outside the United States? (2) Is the target within the categories of targets certified by the Attorney General and the DNI for collection under section 702?
- Section 702 requires the Attorney General and the DNI to provide semiannual assessments of the implementation of section 702 both to the oversight committees in Congress and to the FISC.
- The Inspector General of any intelligence agency that conducts an acquisition under section 702 must regularly review the agency's use of section 702 and provide copies of that review to the Attorney General, the DNI, and the congressional oversight committees.
- The head of any intelligence agency that conducts an acquisition under section 702 must perform an annual review of the agency's implementation of section 702 and provide copies of that review to the FISC, the Attorney General, the DNI, and the congressional oversight committees.
- The Attorney General must make semiannual reports to the congressional intelligence and judiciary committees on the implementation of section 702.
- The Attorney General must make semiannual reports to the congressional intelligence and judiciary committees that include summaries of all significant legal decisions made by the FISC and copies of all decisions, orders, or opinions of the FISC that involve a significant interpretation of any provision of FISA, including section 702.

- The FISC requires the intelligence agencies to immediately report to the court any compliance incidents and the government reports quarterly to the FISC about the status of any previously reported compliance issues.
- An annual Inspector General assessment is provided to Congress reporting on compliance issues, the number of disseminations relating to United States persons, and the number of targets found to be located inside the United States.

In 2012, Senator Diane Feinstein (D-CA), the Chair of the Senate Select Committee on Intelligence, reported that a review of the assessments, reports, and other information available to the Committee "demonstrate that the government implements [section 702] in a responsible manner with relatively few incidents of non-compliance. Where such incidents have arisen, they have been the inadvertent result of human error or technical defect and have been promptly reported and remedied." Indeed, since the enactment of section 702, the Committee "has not identified a single case in which a government official engaged in a willful effort to circumvent or violate the law."[136]

Although compliance issues under section 702 have been infrequent, they have been vexing when they arise. In one instance, the FISC held that, for technical reasons concerning the manner in which the collection occurred, the minimization procedures that applied to NSA's upstream collection[137] of electronic communications did not satisfy the requirements of either FISA or the Fourth Amendment. This was so because NSA's use of upstream collection often involves the inadvertent acquisition of multi- communication transactions (MCTs),[138] many of which do not fall within the parameters of section 702. Judge John Bates of the FISC noted that the "government's revelations regarding the scope of NSA's upstream collection implicate 50 U.S.C. § 1809(a), which makes it a crime (1) to 'engage[] in electronic surveillance under color of law except as authorized' by statute... ."[139]

Judge Bates observed that "NSA acquires more than two hundred fifty million Internet communications each year pursuant to Section 702" and that the vast majority of those communications are "not at issue here."[140] But, he added, the upstream collection represents "approximately 9 percent of the total Internet communications being acquired by NSA under Section 702," and those acquisitions inadvertently sweep in "tens of thousands of wholly domestic communications" because they happen to be contained within an MCT that includes a targeted selector.[141]

In such circumstances, Judge Bates noted that the "fact that NSA's technical measures cannot prevent NSA from acquiring transactions containing wholly domestic communications ... does not render NSA's acquisition of those transactions 'unintentional.'"[142] Judge Bates concluded that "NSA's minimization procedures, as applied to MCTs," did not meet the requirements of either FISA or the Fourth Amendment. He therefore refused to approve NSA's continuing acquisition of MCTs.[143] Thereafter, the government substantially revised its procedures for handling MCTs, and in November 2011 Judge Bates approved the future acquisition of such communications subject to the new minimization standards.[144] In addition, NSA took the additional step of deleting all previously acquired upstream communications.

According to NSA, section 702 "is the most significant tool in NSA collection arsenal for the detection, identification, and disruption of terrorist threats to the US and around the world." To cite just one example, collection under section 702 "was critical to the discovery and disruption" of a planned bomb attack in 2009 against the New York City subway system" and led to the arrest and conviction of Najibullah Zazi and several of his co-conspirators.[145]

According to the Department of Justice and the Office of the Director of National Intelligence in a 2012 report to Congress:

> Section 702 enables the Government to collect information effectively and efficiently about foreign targets overseas and in a manner that protects the privacy and civil liberties of Americans. Through rigorous oversight, the Government is able to evaluate whether changes are needed to the procedures or guidelines, and what other steps may be appropriate to safeguard the privacy of personal information. In addition, the Department of Justice provides the joint assessments and other reports to the FISC. The FISC has been actively involved in the review of section 702 collection. Together, all of these mechanisms ensure thorough and continuous oversight of section 702 activities... .
>
> Section 702 is vital to keeping the nation safe. It provides information about the plans and identities of terrorists, allowing us to glimpse inside terrorist organizations and obtain information about how those groups function and receive support. In addition, it lets us collect information about the intentions and capabilities of weapons proliferators and other foreign adversaries who threaten the United States.[146]

In reauthorizing section 702 for an additional five years in 2012, the Senate Select Committee on Intelligence concluded:

> [T]he authorities provided [under section 702] have greatly increased the government's ability to collect information and act quickly against important foreign intelligence targets. The Committee has also found that [section 702] has been implemented with attention to protecting the privacy and civil liberties of US persons, and has been the subject of extensive oversight by the Executive branch, the FISC, as well as the Congress... . [The] failure to reauthorize [section 702] would "result in a loss of significant intelligence and impede the ability of the Intelligence Community to respond quickly to new threats and intelligence opportunities."[147]

Our own review is not inconsistent with this assessment. During the course of our analysis, NSA shared with the Review Group the details of 54 counterterrorism investigations since 2007 that resulted in the prevention of terrorist attacks in diverse nations and the United States. In all but one of these cases, information obtained under section 702 contributed in some degree to the success of the investigation. Although it is difficult to assess precisely how many of these investigations would have turned out differently without the information learned through section 702, we are persuaded that section 702 does in fact play an important role in the nation's effort to prevent terrorist attacks across the globe.

Although section 702 has clearly served an important function in helping the United States to uncover and prevent terrorist attacks both in the United States and around the world (and thus helps protect our allies), the question remains whether it achieves that goal in a way that unnecessarily sacrifices individual privacy and damages foreign relations. Because the effect of section 702 on United States persons is different from its effect on non-United States persons, it is necessary to examine this question separately for each of these categories of persons.

C. Privacy Protections for United States Persons Whose Communications are Intercepted under Section 702

Recommendation 12: We recommend that, if the government legally intercepts a communication under section 702, or under any other authority that justifies the interception of a communication on the ground that it is directed at a non-United States person who is located outside the United States, and if the communication either includes a United States person as a participant or reveals information about a United States person:

(1) any information about that United States person should be purged upon detection unless it either has foreign intelligence value or is necessary to prevent serious harm to others;
(2) any information about the United States person may not be used in evidence in any proceeding against that United States person;
(3) the government may not search the contents of communications acquired under section 702, or under any other authority covered by this recommendation, in an effort to identify communications of particular United States persons, except (a) when the information is necessary to prevent a threat of death or serious bodily harm, or (b) when the government obtains a warrant based on probable cause to believe that the United States person is planning or is engaged in acts of international terrorism.

Section 702 affords United States persons the same protection against foreign intelligence surveillance when they are outside the United States that FISA affords them when they are inside the United States. That is, a United States person may not lawfully be targeted for foreign intelligence surveillance unless the FISC issues a warrant based on a finding that there is probable cause to believe that the targeted United States person is an agent of a foreign power (as defined in FISA).

Section 702 has a potentially troubling impact on the privacy of communications of United States persons because of the risk of *inadvertent interception*. The government cannot lawfully target the communications of a United States person, whether she is inside or outside the United States, without satisfying the *probable cause* requirements of both FISA and the Fourth Amendment. But in determining whether the target of any particular interception is a non-United States person who is located outside the United States, section 702 requires only that the government *reasonably believe* the target to be such a person. Because United States persons are appreciably more likely to have their constitutionally protected communications *inadvertently* intercepted under the reasonable belief standard than under the probable cause standard, the reasonable belief standard provides less protection to US persons than ordinarily would be the case.

Exacerbating that concern is the risk of *incidental interception*. This occurs when the government acquires the communications of a legally targeted individual under section 702 who is communicating with United States persons who cannot themselves be lawfully targeted for surveillance. The issue of incidental acquisition can arise whenever the government engages in electronic surveillance.

For example, if the government has probable cause to wiretap an individual's phone because he is suspected of dealing drugs, it may incidentally intercept the suspect's conversations with completely innocent persons who happen to speak with the suspect during the duration of the wiretap. In such circumstances, the standard practice in criminal law enforcement is for the government to purge from its records any reference to the innocent person unless it reveals evidence of criminal conduct by the innocent person or provides relevant information about the guilt or innocence of the suspect.[148]

Following a similar approach, when incidental acquisition occurs in the course of section 702 surveillance, existing minimization procedures require that any intercepted communication with a United States person, and any information obtained about a United States person in the course of a section 702 acquisition, must be destroyed—unless it has foreign intelligence value, indicates an imminent threat of death or serious bodily harm, or is evidence of a crime.[149]

In our view, this approach does not adequately protect the legitimate privacy interests of United States persons when their communications are *incidentally* acquired under section 702. This is so for three reasons. First, when a United States person (whether inside or outside the United States) communicates with a legally targeted non-United States person who is outside the United States, there is a significantly greater risk that his communication will be acquired under section 702 than (a) if they communicated with one another when they were both inside the United States or (b) if FISA treated non-United States persons outside the United States the same way it treats United States persons outside the United States. Thus, when an American in Chicago e-mails a foreign friend abroad, there is a significantly greater chance that his e-mail will be acquired under 702 than if he e-mails an American in Paris or a foreigner in New York. This is so because section 702 allows the government to target the foreign friend abroad under a lower standard than if the target was the American in Paris or the foreigner in New York. For this reason, incidental interception is significantly more likely to occur when the interception takes place under section 702 than in other circumstances.

Second, it is often difficult to determine whether the e-mail address, Internet communication, or telephone number of the non-targeted participant in a legally acquired communication belongs to a United States person, because that information often is not apparent on the face of the communication. In such circumstances, there is a significant risk that communications involving United States persons will not be purged and, instead, will be retained in a government database.

Third, the very concept of information of "foreign intelligence value" has a degree of vagueness and can easily lead to the preservation of private information about even known United States persons whose communications are incidentally intercepted in the course of a legal section 702 interception.

For all of these reasons, there is a risk that, after the government incidentally collects communications of or about United States persons in the course of legal section 702 acquisitions, it will later be able to search through its database of communications in a way that invades the legitimate privacy interests of United States persons. Because the underlying rationale of section 702 is that United States persons are entitled to the full protection of their privacy even when they communicate with non-United States persons who are outside the United States, they should not lose that protection merely because the government has legally targeted non-United States persons who are located outside the United States *under a standard that could not legally be employed to target a United States person who participates in that communication*. The privacy interests of United States persons in such circumstances should be accorded substantial protection, particularly because section 702 is not designed or intended to acquire the communications of United States persons.

Our recommended approach would leave the government free to use section 702 to obtain the type of information it is designed and intended to acquire—information about non-United States persons who are the legal targets of these investigations, while at the same time (a) more fully preserving the privacy of United States persons who are *not* the targets of these interceptions and (b) reducing the incentive the government might otherwise have to use section 702 in an effort to gather evidence against United States persons in a way that would circumvent the underlying values of both FISA and the Fourth Amendment.[150]

D. Privacy Protections for Non-United States Persons

***Recommendation 13*:** We recommend that, in implementing section 702, and any other authority that authorizes the surveillance of non-United States persons who are outside the United States, in addition to the safeguards and oversight mechanisms already in place, the US Government should reaffirm that such surveillance:

(1) must be authorized by duly enacted laws or properly authorized executive orders;
(2) must be directed *exclusively* at the national security of the United States or our allies;
(3) must *not* be directed at illicit or illegitimate ends, such as the theft of trade secrets or obtaining commercial gain for domestic industries; and
(4) must not disseminate information about non-United States persons if the information is not relevant to protecting the national security of the United States or our allies.

In addition, the US Government should make clear that such surveillance:

(1) must not target any non-United States person located outside of the United States based solely on that person's political views or religious convictions; and
(2) must be subject to careful oversight and to the highest degree of transparency consistent with protecting the national security of the United States and our allies.

Because section 702 is directed specifically at non-United States persons, it raises the question whether it sufficiently respects the legitimate privacy interests of such persons. At the outset, it is important to note that, when non-citizens are *inside* the United States, our law accords them the full protection of the Fourth Amendment. They have the same right to be free of unreasonable searches and seizures as American citizens. Moreover, non-citizens who have made a commitment to our community by establishing legal residence in the United States are designated "United State persons" and, as such, are treated the same way as American citizens in terms of government surveillance—even when they are *outside* the United States. These are important protections for individuals who are not citizens of the United States.

What, though, of *non-United States* persons who are *outside* the United States? We begin by emphasizing that, contrary to some representations, section 702 does *not* authorize NSA to acquire the content of the communications of masses of ordinary people. To the contrary, section 702 authorizes NSA to intercept communications of non-United States persons who are outside the United States *only* if it reasonably believes that a particular "identifier" (for example, an e-mail address or a telephone number) is being used to communicate foreign intelligence information related to such matters as international terrorism, nuclear proliferation, or hostile cyber activities. NSA's determinations are subjected to constant, ongoing, and independent review by all three branches of the federal government to ensure that NSA targets *only* identifiers that meet these criteria.

That still leaves the question, however, whether section 702 adequately respects the legitimate privacy interests of non-United States persons when they are in their home countries or otherwise outside the United States. If section 702 were designed to intercept the communications of United States persons, it would clearly violate the Fourth Amendment.[151] Does it also violate the Fourth Amendment insofar as it is directed at non- United States persons who are located outside the United States? The Supreme Court has definitively answered this question in the negative.[152]

Wholly apart from the Fourth Amendment, how *should* the United States treat non-United States persons when they are outside the United States? To understand the legal distinction between United States persons and non-United States persons, it is important to recognize that the special protections that FISA affords United States persons grew directly out of a distinct and troubling era in American history. In that era, the United States government improperly and sometimes unlawfully targeted American citizens for surveillance in a pervasive and dangerous effort to manipulate domestic political activity in a manner that threatened to undermine the core processes of American democracy. As we have seen, that concern was the driving force behind the enactment of FISA.

Against that background, FISA's especially strict limitations on government surveillance of United States persons reflects not only a respect for individual privacy, but also—and fundamentally—a deep concern about potential government abuse *within our own political system*. The special protections for United States persons must therefore be understood as a crucial safeguard of democratic accountability and effective self-governance within the American political system. In light of that history and those concerns, there is good reason for every nation to enact *special* restrictions on government surveillance of those persons who participate directly in its own system of self-governance.

As an aside, we note that the very existence of these protections in the United States can help promote and preserve democratic accountability across the globe. In light of the global influence of the United States, any threat to effective democracy in the United States could have negative and far-reaching consequences in other nations as well. By helping to maintain an effective system of checks and balances within the United States, the special protections that FISA affords United States persons can therefore contribute to sustaining democratic ideals abroad.

That brings us back, however, to the question of how the United States should treat non-United States persons who are not themselves either a part of our community or physically located in the United States. As a general rule, nations quite understandably treat their own citizens differently than they treat the citizens of other nations. On the other hand, there are sound, indeed, compelling reasons to treat the citizens of other nations with dignity and respect. As President Franklin Delano Roosevelt observed, the United States should be a "good neighbor." Sometimes this is simply a matter of national self-interest. If the United States wants other nations to treat our citizens well, we must treat their citizens well. But there are other reasons for being a "good neighbor."

If we are too aggressive in our surveillance policies under section 702, we might trigger serious economic repercussions for American businesses, which might lose their share of the world's communications market because of a growing distrust of their capacity to guarantee the privacy of their international users. Recent disclosures have generated considerable concern along these lines.

Similarly, unrestrained American surveillance of non-United States persons might alienate other nations, fracture the unity of the Internet, and undermine the free flow of information across national boundaries. This, too, is a serious concern that cuts in favor of restraint.

Perhaps most important, however, is the simple and fundamental issue of respect for personal privacy and human dignity – wherever people may reside. The right of privacy has been recognized as a basic human right that all nations should respect. Both Article 12 of the Universal Declaration of Human Rights and Article 17 of the International Covenant on Civil and Political Rights proclaim that "No one shall be subjected to arbitrary or unlawful interference with his privacy... ." Although that declaration provides little guidance about what is meant by "arbitrary or unlawful interference," the aspiration is clear. The United States should be a leader in championing the protection by all nations of fundamental human rights, including the right of privacy, which is central to human dignity.

At this moment in history, one of the gravest dangers to our national security is international terrorism. Faced with that continuing and grave threat, the United States must find effective ways to identify would-be terrorists who are not located in the United States, who move freely across national borders, and who do everything in their power to mask their identities, intentions, and plans. In such circumstances, the challenge of striking a sound balance between protecting the safety and security of our own citizens and respecting the legitimate interests of the citizens of other nations is especially daunting. Our recommendations have been designed to achieve that balance.

With our recommendations in place, there would be three primary differences between the standards governing the acquisition of communications of United States persons and non-United States persons under section 702 when they are outside the United States. First, United States persons can be targeted only upon a showing of probable cause, whereas non-United States persons can be targeted upon a showing of reasonable belief. Second, United States persons can be targeted only if there is a judicial warrant from the FISC, whereas non-United States persons can be targeted without such a warrant, but with careful after-the- fact review and oversight. Third, the minimization requirements for communications of United States persons would not extend fully to non- United States persons located outside the United States, but importantly, information collected about such persons would not be disseminated unless it is relevant to the national security of the United States or our allies.

In our judgment, these differences are warranted by the *special* obligation the United States Government owes to "the people" of the United States, while at the same time more than upholding our international obligation to ensure that no person "shall be subjected to arbitrary or unlawful interference with his privacy." We encourage all nations to abide by these same limitations.[153]

***Recommendation 14*:** We recommend that, in the absence of a specific and compelling showing, the US Government should follow the model of the Department of Homeland Security, and apply the Privacy Act of 1974 in the same way to both US persons and non-US persons.

The Privacy Act of 1974[154] provides what are known as "privacy fair information practices" for systems of records held by federal agencies. These practices, designed to safeguard personal privacy, include a set of legal requirements meant to ensure both the accuracy and the security of personally identifiable information in a system of records. Perhaps most important, individuals have the right to have access to those records and to make corrections, if needed.

Since its enactment, the Act has applied only to United States persons. In 2009, the Department of Homeland Security (DHS) updated its 2007 "Privacy Policy Guidance Memorandum."[155] This memorandum governs privacy protections for "mixed systems" of records—systems that collect or use information in an identifiable form and that contain information about both United States and non-United States persons.[156]

Today, DHS policy applies the Privacy Act in the same way to both US persons and non-US persons. As stated in the Memorandum, "As a matter of law the Privacy Act ... does not cover visitors or aliens. As a matter of DHS policy, any personally identifiable information (PII) that is collected, used, maintained, and/or disseminated in connection with a mixed system by DHS shall be treated as a System of Records subject to the Privacy Act regardless of whether the information pertains to a US citizen, legal permanent resident, visitor, or alien."[157]

The consequence of this policy is that DHS now handles non-US person PII held in mixed systems in accordance with the fair information practices set forth in the Privacy Act. Non-US persons have the right of access to their PII and the right to amend their records, absent an exemption under the Privacy Act. Because of statutory limitations, the policy does not extend or create a right of judicial review for non-US persons.

Intelligence agencies today are covered by the Privacy Act, with exemptions to accommodate the need to protect matters that are properly classified or law-enforcement sensitive/investigatory in nature. For instance, NSA has filed twenty-six systems of records notices advising the public about data collections, including from applicants seeking employment, contractors doing business with the agency, and in order to conduct background investigations.

NSA also completes privacy impact assessments under the E- Government Act of 2002[158] for its non-National Security Systems that collect, maintain, use, or disseminate PII about members of the public. CIA provides protections under the Privacy Act in contexts including collection directly from the individual; records describing individuals' exercise of First Amendment rights; and the Act's general prohibition on disclosure absent express written consent of the individual. The FBI applies the Privacy Act in the same manner for national security investigations as it does for other records covered by the Act.

Unless the agencies provide specific and persuasive reasons not to do so, we recommend that the DHS policy should be extended to the mixed systems held in intelligence and other federal agencies. DHS policy has existed for several years for major record systems of records, including passenger name records and immigration records, and implementation experience from DHS can guide similar privacy protections for PII held in intelligence and other federal agencies.

Appropriate exception authority appears to exist under the Act, including for National Security Systems and law enforcement investigatory purposes. The previous lack of Privacy Act protections has been a recurring complaint from European and other allies. This reform is manageable based on the DHS experience. It will both affirm the legitimate privacy rights of citizens of other nations and strengthen our relations with allies.

***Recommendation 15*:** We recommend that the National Security Agency should have a limited statutory emergency authority to continue to track known targets of counterterrorism surveillance when they first enter the United States, until the Foreign Intelligence Surveillance Court has time to issue an order authorizing continuing surveillance inside the United States.

Under current law, a problem arises under current law when known targets of counterterrorism surveillance enter the United States. Surveillance of a target has been legally authorized under the standards that apply overseas, under Section 702 or Executive Order 12333. Suddenly, the target is found to be in the United States, where surveillance is permitted only under stricter legal standards. Under current law, NSA must cease collecting information as soon as it determines that the individual is within the United States. The surveillance can begin again only once there is new authorization under FISA. The irony of this outcome is that surveillance must cease at precisely the moment when the target has entered the United States and thus is in position to take hostile action. Colloquially, there can be a costly fumble in the hand-off from overseas to domestic surveillance.

To address this gap in coverage, legislation has been proposed that would amend 50 U.S.C. § 1805 to give the Director of NSA emergency authority to acquire foreign intelligence information in such circumstances for up to 72 hours. We believe that some such authority is appropriate. A similar gap occurs where the target of surveillance overseas was originally thought to be a non-US person and then is found actually to be a US person. At the moment the target is being investigated for counterterrorism purposes, the authorities that permitted the surveillance no longer apply.

The gap in coverage arises due to the different legal standards that apply at home and abroad. Surveillance under Section 702 is permitted if there is a reasonable belief that the person is not a US person and is located outside of the US, and if the purpose is to acquire foreign intelligence information subject to an existing certification. Surveillance under Executive Order 12333 is done so long as it is related to foreign intelligence. By contrast, a traditional FISA order for surveillance within the US requires probable cause that the person is an agent of a foreign power. In order to target a US person who is outside of the US under FISA section 704, the government must show facts for reasonably believing that the person is outside of the US and is an agent of a foreign power. It can take time and effort to upgrade the factual findings from what enabled the surveillance within NSA under Section 702 or Executive Order 12333 to the findings that the Department of Justice needs to meet under a traditional FISA order or one under section 704.

The precise scope of this hand-off authority deserves careful thought. The proposed legislation would allow seventy-two hours for surveillance on order of the NSA Director, followed by additional days of emergency authority by authorization of the Attorney General. There has been discussion of whether to limit the scope to situations where there is an imminent threat of death or serious bodily harm, or to go somewhat broader and allow the hand-off authority for any counterterrorism investigation. Additional facts and public discussion would be helpful to assessing such questions.

However these questions of scope are resolved, it can be difficult in our era of mobile phones and e-mail addresses to determine when a communication is made within the United

States. Where the communication unexpectedly is within our borders, or someone thought to be a non-US person is found to be a US person, there should be a capacity to respond to an emergency situation.

SECTION V. DETERMINING WHAT INTELLIGENCE SHOULD BE COLLECTED AND HOW

The United States led the defense of the Free World in the Cold War. After having been targeted by terrorist groups, it led the global community's efforts to combat violent extremism. Over time, the United States has developed a large Intelligence Community with unparalleled collection capabilities. The Intelligence Community collects information essential not only to our national security but also to that of many allied and friendly nations. The unsurpassed prowess of US technical intelligence collection is a major component of the maintenance of peace and security of the United States and many other nations.

Intelligence collection is designed to inform policymakers, warfighters, and law enforcement officers who are responsible for making decisions and taking actions to protect the United States and its allies. Intelligence collection is not an end in itself. Intelligence collection should not occur because it is possible, but only because it is *necessary*.

Intelligence, particularly signals intelligence, is as necessary now as ever to combat violent extremism, prevent the proliferation of nuclear weapons, combat international criminal groups, prevent atrocities, and enforce UN sanctions and other international regimes. With the passage of a dozen years since the attacks of September 11, 2001, the threat from al-Qa'ida and similar groups has changed, but it remains significant. For example, recent years have seen the spread of al-Qa'ida-related groups to large swaths of Africa and the Middle East. We have also witnessed a rise in "Lone Wolf" terrorism, including in the United States. There is a continuing need for appropriate intelligence collection, data analysis, and information-sharing with appropriate personnel. So, too, there is a need for appropriate controls and oversight on intelligence collection to ensure that we act in ways that are both consistent with our values and reflective of our security requirements.

To ascertain those requirements, the US Government has created a process known as the National Intelligence Priorities Framework (NIPF). While this process to produce intelligence priorities is the most robust ever used by the Intelligence Community, we believe that the NIPF system can and should be strengthened to ensure that what we seek to collect is truly needed and that our methods of collection are consistent with our values and policies.

A. Priorities and Appropriateness

To ascertain what intelligence is necessary to collect, policy officials and intelligence officers interact to establish intelligence needs or requirements and then priorities within those requirements. This process has been formalized into the NIPF.

The NIPF divides all intelligence collection needs identified by policymakers into five categories or tiers in increasing degrees of importance. Tiers One and Two reflect the priorities of the nation, as articulated by the President, following priority identification and review by sub-Cabinet-level officials in the National Security Council (NSC) Deputies Committee and then by Cabinet-level officials in the NSC Principals Committee. Tiers Three, Four, and Five reflect information needed by other government agencies and programs to carry out their legal mandates. The review process for Tiers Three through Five is coordinated by the Director of National Intelligence and involves policy officials at levels below the Principals and Deputies.

The NIPF is reviewed, approved, and issued annually. Once an intelligence priority is approved, it is converted into a specific collection plan. Coordination of the collection is conducted by the Office of the Director of National Intelligence.

Many intelligence priorities result in collection on a global basis. For example, an intelligence priority to monitor al-Qa'ida threats may mean collecting information not only in Afghanistan and Pakistan, where al- Qa'ida is headquartered, but also in scores of nations to which al-Qa'ida and its supporters have moved or emerged and which they might threaten.

Enforcement of UN and other sanctions, stopping the proliferation of materials needed for nuclear weapons, halting the trafficking in persons, combating illicit drugs and criminal cartels, reducing the risk of mass atrocities, detecting the systematic violation of ethnic minority rights, and the detection of war crimes are all examples of intelligence priorities that require the collection of information in many nations. Often other governments will not have the ability to collect information on these requirements within their borders. Sometimes, they will intentionally seek to deny the international community information about these concerns. The United States regularly shares information about these issues with allied and cooperating governments, and with international organizations.

The United States is hardly alone in collecting such intelligence. Most nations collect intelligence, often limited only by their ability and resources. Indeed, the United States is an intelligence collection target of many nations, including friendly and even allied countries. The President's own communications are a collection target for many nations, friendly and otherwise.

One thing that makes United States intelligence collection unique is the degree of oversight and control by high-level officials, elected legislative members, and the judiciary (see Appendix C). No other intelligence services in the world are subjected to the degree of policy, legislative, and judicial review now applied to the US Intelligence Community. In our view, however, that oversight can be improved. The current NIPF process does not provide sufficient high-level oversight of a) lower-tier priorities; b) the specific means used to collect information on a priority; c) the locations where collection on a priority may occur; and d) developments that occur between annual reviews.

This NIPF process should be strengthened to assure that sensitive collection is undertaken only after consideration of all national interests and with the participation of those officials who have responsibility for those interests. The following should be added to the process: (1) senior- level "interagency" policy oversight of *all* sensitive requirements, rather than only the requirements in Tier One and Tier Two; (2) participation in the process by all the departments and agencies with relevant concerns, including economic ones; and (3) senior-level knowledge of and approval of specific targets of collection whenever the target or collection means is a sensitive one. We discuss below what constitutes a "sensitive" collection activity.

The rationale behind these recommendations is simple. Senior policymakers should determine the activities of intelligence agencies; senior policymakers are the only participants with the breadth of experience to make such decisions; and any senior policymaker with relevant expertise and perspective should participate in policy formulation on sensitive collection.

B. Monitoring Sensitive Collection

***Recommendation 16*:** We recommend that the President should create a new process requiring high-level approval of all sensitive intelligence requirements and the methods the Intelligence Community will use to meet them. This process should, among other things, identify both the uses and limits of surveillance on foreign leaders and in foreign nations. A small staff of policy and intelligence professionals should review intelligence collection for sensitive activities on an ongoing basis throughout the year and advise the National Security Council Deputies and Principals when they believe that an unscheduled review by them may be warranted.

***Recommendation 17*:** We recommend that:

(1) senior policymakers should review not only the requirements in Tier One and Tier Two of the National Intelligence Priorities Framework, but also any other requirements that they define as sensitive;
(2) senior policymakers should review the methods and targets of collection on requirements in any Tier that they deem sensitive; and
(3) senior policymakers from the federal agencies with responsibility for US economic interests should participate in the review process because disclosures of classified information can have detrimental effects on US economic interests.

***Recommendation 18*:** We recommend that the Director of National Intelligence should establish a mechanism to monitor the collection and dissemination activities of the Intelligence Community to ensure they are consistent with the determinations of senior policymakers. To this end, the Director of National Intelligence should prepare an annual report on this issue to the National Security Advisor, to be shared with the Congressional intelligence committees.

We believe that the definition of what is "sensitive," and therefore should be reviewed in this strengthened NIPF, will vary with time. Among the factors that might make something sufficiently "sensitive" to require senior interagency-level review are 1) the means that would be employed to collect information, 2) the specific people subject to collection, 3) the nation where the collection would occur, 4) international events such as a head-of-state meeting or negotiations, or 5) a combination of these factors.

Intelligence collection managers may not always be aware that what they are doing or planning might fall into a category that makes it sensitive in the eyes of policymakers. Senior policymakers may not be aware that a collection effort they previously approved has become "sensitive" over time.

We recommend that a standing group or office should review collection activities for "sensitive" activities on an ongoing basis. This Sensitive Activities Office should include both policymakers and intelligence collection managers, assigned perhaps for 12-18 month rotations. The Sensitive Activities Office would nominate collection efforts for senior-level consideration if necessary between annual NIPF reviews.

The Sensitive Activities Office should include staff from non- traditional national security organizations such as the National Economic Council, Treasury, Commerce, and the Trade Representative. In addition, any department should be able to request a review of ongoing intelligence collection by the Sensitive Activities Office at any time, in light of new developments or evolving situations of which they are aware. The Sensitive Activities Office should be housed and supported by the ODNI, but should report regularly, through the DNI, to a policy-level official in the National Security Staff (NSS).

The goal of this strengthened NIPF is to ensure that the United States collects all of the information it legitimately needs and as little more than that as possible, and that we collect not because we can, but because we must for our national security, that of our allies, and in support of the international community.

Toward that end, the Principals reviewing intelligence collection should re-institute use of the so-called "Front-Page Rule." That informal precept, long employed by the leaders of US administrations, is that we should not engage in any secret, covert, or clandestine activity if we could not persuade the American people of the necessity and wisdom of such activities were they to learn of them as the result of a leak or other disclosure. The corollary of that rule is that if a foreign government's likely negative reaction to a revealed collection effort would outweigh the value of the information likely to be obtained, then do not do it.

C. Leadership Intentions

***Recommendation 19*:** We recommend that decisions to engage in surveillance of foreign leaders should consider the following criteria:

(1) Is there a need to engage in such surveillance in order to assess significant threats to our national security?
(2) Is the other nation one with whom we share values and interests, with whom we have a cooperative relationship, and whose leaders we should accord a high degree of respect and deference?
(3) Is there a reason to believe that the foreign leader may be being duplicitous in dealing with senior US officials or is attempting to hide information relevant to national security concerns from the US?
(4) Are there other collection means or collection targets that could reliably reveal the needed information?
(5) What would be the negative effects if the leader became aware of the US collection, or if citizens of the relevant nation became so aware?

The United States, like all governments, seeks to learn the real intentions of leaders of many nations. Historically, some national leaders may have told the United States one thing in diplomatic channels, and then secretly ordered a very different set of actions. Often the "easiest" way to determine or verify intentions may seem to be to monitor leadership communications.

We believe, however, that any decision to engage in surveillance of the leaders of a foreign nation must be taken with great care. For a variety of reasons, the stakes in such decisions can be quite high. Although general principles may not themselves resolve close and difficult cases, they can help to ensure a proper focus on the relevant considerations and a degree of consistency in our judgments. Here as elsewhere, risk management is central. The decision to engage in surveillance of foreign leaders must address and manage multiple risks.

The first task in this inquiry must be to consider the various purposes for which such information might be sought. In some instances, information might be sought in order to reduce significant risks to national security or to learn the views of foreign leaders regarding critical national security issues, where those views have not been shared with the United States. In other instances, information might be sought in order to learn about the intentions of the leaders of other nations, even when no threat to our national security is involved. The latter instances might involve an interest in acquiring information that might prove useful as United States officials plan for meetings and discussions with other nations on bilateral economic issues. In such circumstances, it might be helpful to know in advance about another nation's internal concerns and priorities or about its planned negotiating strategy but it is not critical to national security. Different interests have different weights.

The second task is to consider the nations from whom information might be collected. In some instances, we might seek to collect information from the leaders of nations with whom the United States has a hostile relationship. Other nations are our friends and allies, and we may have close and supportive relationships with them.

In making judgments about whether to engage in surveillance of foreign leaders, we suggest that these questions should be considered: (1) Is there a need to engage in such surveillance in order to assess significant threats to our national security? (2) Is the other nation one with whom we share values and interests, with whom we have a cooperative relationship, and whose leaders we should accord a high degree of respect and deference? (3) Is there a reason to believe the foreign leader may be being duplicitous in dealing with senior US officials or is attempting to hide information relevant to national security concerns from the US? (4) Are there other collection means or collection targets that could reliably reveal the needed information? (5) What would be the negative effects if the leader became aware of the US collection, or if citizens of the relevant nation became so aware? These questions can helpfully orient sensitive judgments.

***Recommendation 20*:** We recommend that the US Government should examine the feasibility of creating software that would allow the National Security Agency and other intelligence agencies more easily to conduct targeted information acquisition rather than bulk-data collection.

In the course of our review, we have been struck by the fact that the nature of IT networks and current intelligence collection technology is such that it is often necessary to ingest large amounts of data in order to acquire a limited amount of required data. E-mails, telephone calls, and other communications are moved on networks as a series of small packets, then reassembled at the receiving end. Often those packets are interspersed in transit with packets from different originators. To intercept one message, pieces of many other messages might be recorded and placed in government databases, at least temporarily. Frequently, too, it is more cost-effective and less likely to be detected by the transmitter if the collection of a message occurs in transit, mixed up with many others, rather than at the source.

It might reduce budgetary costs and political risk if technical collection agencies could make use of artificial intelligence software that could be launched onto networks and would be able to determine in real time what precise information packets should be collected. Such smart software would be making the sorting decision online, as distinguished from the current situation in which vast amounts of data are swept up and the sorting is done after it has been copied on to data storages systems. We are unable to determine whether this concept is feasible or fantasy, but we suggest that it should be examined by an interagency information technology research team.

D. Cooperation with Our Allies

Recommendation 21**:** We recommend that with a small number of closely allied governments, meeting specific criteria, the US Government should explore understandings or arrangements regarding intelligence collection guidelines and practices with respect to each others' citizens (including, if and where appropriate, intentions, strictures, or limitations with respect to collections). The criteria should include:

(1) shared national security objectives;
(2) a close, open, honest, and cooperative relationship between senior-level policy officials; and
(3) a relationship between intelligence services characterized both by the sharing of intelligence information and analytic thinking and by operational cooperation against critical targets of joint national security concern. Discussions of such understandings or arrangements should be done between relevant intelligence communities, with senior policy-level oversight.

We suggest that the US Government should work with closely allied nations to explore understanding or arrangements regarding intelligence collection guidelines and practices with respect to each others' citizens. It is important to emphasize that the United States has not entered into formal agreements with other nations not to collect information on each others' citizens. There are no such formal agreements. With a very small number of governments, however, there are bilateral arrangements or understandings on this issue (which include, in appropriate cases, intentions, strictures, and limitations with respect to collection). These bilateral relationships are based on decades of familiarity, transparency, and past performance between the relevant policy and intelligence communities.

The United States should be willing to explore the possibility of reaching similar arrangements and understandings with a small number of other closely allied governments. Such relationships should be entered into with care and require senior policy-level involvement. We anticipate that only a very few new such relationships are likely in the short to medium term.

In choosing with which nations to have such discussions, the US Government should have explicit criteria in mind and should share those criteria with interested governments. The criteria should include (1) shared national security policy objectives between the two governments; (2) a close, open, and honest relationship between the policy officials of the two nations; and (3) a close working relationships between the countries' intelligence services, including the sharing of a broad range of intelligence information; analytic and operational cooperation involving intelligence targets of common interest; and the ability to handle intelligence information with great care.

The US Government has indicated that it is considering disclosing publicly the procedures that the Intelligence Community follows in the handling of foreign intelligence information it collects pertaining to non-US persons. We encourage the Government to make such procedures known. The individual agencies' performance in implementing these procedures should be overseen both by the Director of National Intelligence—with regular reports to senior-level policy officials—and by the two Congressional Intelligence Committees.

SECTION VI. ORGANIZATIONAL REFORM IN LIGHT OF CHANGING COMMUNICATIONS TECHNOLOGY

A. Introduction

A central theme of this Report is the importance of achieving multiple goals, including: (1) combating threats to the national security; (2) protecting other national security and foreign policy interests; (3) assuring fundamental rights to privacy; (4) preserving democracy, civil liberties, and the rule of law; (5) supporting a robust, innovative, and free Internet; and (6) protecting strategic relationships. This section identifies organizational structures designed to achieve these goals in light of changes in communications technology.

For reasons deeply rooted in the history of the intelligence enterprise, the current organizational structure has been overwhelmingly focused on the goal of combating threats to national security. NSA grew out of signals intelligence efforts during World War II. From then until the end of the Cold War, NSA targeted its efforts on nation states, outside of the US, often in foreign combat zones that were distant from home.

By contrast, our intelligence efforts now target nonstate actors, including terrorist organizations for whom borders are often not an obstacle. As the Section 215 program illustrates, the traditional distinction between foreign and domestic has become less clear. The distinction between military and civilian has also become less clear, now that the same communications devices, software, and networks are used both in war zones such as Iraq and Afghanistan and in the rest of the world. Similarly, the distinction between war and non-war is less clear, as the United States stays vigilant against daily cyber security attacks as well as other threats from abroad.

The organizational structure of the Intelligence Community should reflect these changes. Today, communications devices, software, and networks are often "dual-use"—used for both military and civilian purposes. Both military and civilian goals are thus implicated by signals intelligence and surveillance of communications systems. Section V addressed the need for a new policy process to oversee sensitive intelligence collections, drawing on multiple federal agencies and multiple national goals. This section identifies key organizational changes, including:

- Re-organization of NSA to refocus the agency on its core mission of foreign intelligence;
- Creation of a new Civil Liberties and Privacy Protection Board (CLPP Board) to expand beyond the statutory limits of the existing Privacy and Civil Liberties Oversight Board (PCLOB); and
- Changes to the FISC to create a Public Interest Advocate, increase transparency, and improve the appointment process.

B. The National Security Agency

We recommend major changes to the structure of the National Security Agency. There should be greater civilian control over the agency, including Senate confirmation for the Director and openness to having a civilian Director. NSA should refocus on its core function: the collection and use of foreign intelligence information. To distinguish the warfighting role from the intelligence role, the military Cyber-Command should not be led by the NSA Director. Because the defense of both civilian and government cyber-systems has become more important in recent years, we recommend splitting the defensive mission of NSA's Information Assurance Directorate into a separate organization.

Before discussing these recommendations, we offer some general observations. No other organization in the world has the breadth and depth of capabilities NSA possesses; its prowess in the realm of signals intelligence is extraordinary. Since World War II, NSA and its predecessors have worked to keep our nation and our allies safe from attack. SIGINT collected by NSA is used daily to support our warfighters and to combat terrorism, the proliferation of weapons of mass destruction, and international criminal and narcotics cartels. Its successes make it possible for the United States and our allies around the world to safeguard our citizens and prevent death, disaster, and destruction.

In addition to its leading-edge technological developments and operations, NSA employs large numbers of highly trained, qualified, and professional staff. The hard work and dedication to mission of NSA's work force is apparent. NSA has increased the staff in its compliance office and addressed many concerns expressed previously by the FISC and others.

After the terrorist acts in the United States of September 11, 2001, many people in both the Legislative and Executive Branches of government believed that substantial new measures were needed to protect our national security. We have noted that if a similar or worse incident or series of attacks were to occur in the future, many Americans, in the fear and heat of the moment, might support new restrictions on civil liberties and privacy. The powerful existing and potential capabilities of our intelligence and law enforcement agencies might be unleashed without adequate controls. Once unleashed, it could be difficult to roll back these sacrifices of freedom.

Our recommendations about NSA are designed in part to create checks and balances that would make it more difficult in the future to impose excessive government surveillance. Of course, no structural reforms create perfect safeguards. But it is possible to make restraint more likely. Vigilance is required in every age to maintain liberty.

1. "Dual-Use" Technologies: The Convergence of Civilian Communications and Intelligence Collection

Our recommended organizational changes are informed by the recent history of communications technologies. For the most part, signals intelligence during World War II and the Cold War did not involve collection and use on the equipment and networks used by ordinary Americans. Signals intelligence today, by contrast, pervasively involves the communications devices, software, and networks that are also used by ordinary Americans and citizens of other countries. When the equipment and networks were separate, there was relatively little reason for decisions about signals intelligence to be part of a wide-ranging policy inquiry into the interest of the United States. But when the devices, software, and networks are the same as those used by ordinary Americans (and ordinary citizens of other countries), then multiple and significant policy concerns come into play.

As a result of changing technology, key distinctions about intelligence and communications technology have eroded over time: state vs. nonstate, foreign vs. domestic, war vs. non-war, and military vs. civilian. As a result, many communications technologies today are "dual- use"—used for both civilian and military purposes. For ordinary civilians, this means that our daily communications get swept up into Intelligence Community databases. For the military, it means that what used to be purely military activities often now have important effects on private citizens.

1. ***From nation-states to well-hidden terrorists.*** During the Cold War, our intelligence efforts were directed against foreign powers, notably the Soviet Union, and agents of foreign powers, such as Soviet agents in the US who were placed under FISA wiretap orders. After the terrorist attacks of September 11, 2001, the emphasis shifted to fighting terrorism. In counterterrorism efforts, a major priority is to identify potential or actual terrorists, who seek to hide their communications in the vast sea of other communications.

   The Section 215 telephone database, for instance, was designed to find links between suspected terrorists and previously unknown threats. It is one of many databases created after the terrorist attacks of September 11, 2001 in order to "connect the dots" and discover terrorist threats. One result of the focus on counterterrorism has been that the Intelligence Community has broadened its focus from state actors to a large number of nonstate actors. Another result is that the communications of ordinary citizens are placed into intelligence databases, increasing the effects of SIGINT policy choices on individuals and businesses.
2. ***From domestic to foreign.*** For ordinary citizens, the distinction between domestic and foreign communications has eroded over time. As the Director of National Intelligence, General James Clapper, has testified before Congress,[159] much of the intelligence collection during the Cold War occurred in separate communications systems. Behind the Iron Curtain, the communications of the Soviet Union and its allies were largely separate from other nations. Direct communications from ordinary Americans to Communist nations were a tiny fraction of electronic communications. By contrast, the Internet is global. Terrorists and their allies use the same Internet as ordinary Americans.

   During the Cold War, ordinary Americans used the telephone for many local calls, but they were cautious about expensive "long-distance" calls to other area codes and were even more cautious about the especially expensive "international" phone calls. Many people today, by contrast, treat the idea of "long-distance" or "international" calls as a relic of the past. We make international calls through purchases of inexpensive phone cards or free global video services. International e-mails are cost-free for users.

The pervasively international nature of communications today was the principal rationale for creating Section 702 and other parts of the FISA Amendments Act of 2008. In addition, any communication on the Internet might be routed through a location outside of the United States, in which case FISA does not apply and collection is governed under broader authorities such as Executive Order 12333. Today, and unbeknownst to US users, websites and cloud servers may be located outside the United States. Even for a person in the US who never knowingly sends communications abroad, there may be collection by US intelligence agencies outside of the US. [160] The cross-border nature of today's communications suggests that when decisions are made about foreign surveillance, there is a need for greater consideration of policy goals involving the protection of civilian commerce and individual privacy.

3. ***From wartime to continuous responses to cyber and other threats.*** In recent decades, the global nature of the Internet has enabled daily cyber- attacks on the communications of government, business, and ordinary Americans by hackers, organized crime, terrorists, and nation-states. As a result, the development of high-quality defenses against such attacks has become a priority for civilian as well as military systems. In wartime, the military anticipates that the adversary will try to jam communications and take other measures to interfere with its ability to carry out operations. For this reason, the military has long required an effective defensive capability for its communications, called an "information assurance" capability. With cyber-attacks, often launched from overseas, information assurance now is needed outside the military context as well.

   The convergence of military and civilian systems for cyber security has three implications. First, information assurance for the military relies increasingly on information assurance in the civilian sector. With the use of commercial off-the-shelf hardware and software, many military systems are now the same as or similar to civilian systems. The military and the US Government rely on a broad range of critical infrastructure, which is mostly owned and operated by the civilian sector. Effective defense of civilian-side hardware, software, and infrastructure is critical to military and other government functions.

   Second, the military chain of command does not apply to the civilian sector. For traditional information assurance, the military could depend on its own personnel and systems to fix communications problems caused by the adversary—the military could secretly order its personnel how to respond to a problem. But that sort of chain of command does not work in the civilian sector, where patches and other defensive measures must be communicated to a multitude of civilian system owners. It is usually not possible to communicate effective defensive measures without also tipping off adversaries about our vulnerabilities and responses.

   Third, these changes create a greater tension between offense and defense. When the military can keep secrets within the chain of command, then the offensive measures used in intelligence collection or cyber attacks can safely go forward. The offense remains useful, and the military can defend its own systems. Where there is no chain of command, however, there is no secret way for the defenders to patch their systems. Those charged with offensive responsibilities still seek to collect SIGINT or carry out cyber attacks. By contrast, those charged with information assurance have no effective way to protect the multitude of exposed systems from the attacks. The SIGINT function and the information assurance function conflict more fundamentally than before. This conclusion supports our recommendation to split the Information Assurance Directorate of NSA into a separate organization.

4. ***From military combat zones to civilian communications.*** An important change, which has received relatively little attention, concerns the military significance of the communications devices, software, and networks used by ordinary Americans. In certain ways the military nature of signals intelligence is well known—NSA is part of the Department of Defense (DOD), the current Director of NSA is a general, and the military's Cyber Command is led by the same general. Much less appreciated are (1) the possible effect that active combat operations in Iraq and Afghanistan have had on decisions about what intelligence activities are appropriate and (2) the increasing overlap between signals intelligence for military purposes and the communications of ordinary Americans and citizens of other countries.

   The convergence of military and civilian communications is important in light of the drastically different expectations of government surveillance. In wartime, during active military operations, signals intelligence directed at the enemy must be highly aggressive and largely unrestrained. The United States and its allies gained vital military intelligence during World War II by breaking German and Japanese codes. During the Cold War, the United States established listening stations on the edges of the Soviet Union in order to intercept communications. More recently, there are powerful arguments for strong measures to intercept communications to prevent or detect attacks on American troops in Iraq and Afghanistan. During military operations, the goal is information dominance, to protect the lives and safety of US forces and to meet military objectives. The same rules do not apply on the home front.

   A significant challenge today is that a wide and increasing range of communications technologies is used in both military and civilian settings. The same mobile phones, laptops, and other consumer goods used in combat zones are often used in the rest of the world. The same is true for software, such as operating systems, encryption protocols, and applications. Similarly, routers, fiber optic, and other networking features link combat zones with the rest of the global Internet. Today, no battlefield lines or Iron Curtain separates the communications in combat zones from the rest of the world. A vulnerability that can be exploited on the battlefield can also be exploited elsewhere. The policy challenge is how to achieve our military goals in combat zones without undermining the privacy and security of our communications elsewhere. In responding to this challenge, it remains vital to allow vigorous pursuit of military goals in combat zones and to avoid creating a chilling effect on the actions of our armed forces there.

   The public debate has generally focused on the counterterrorism rationale for expanded surveillance since the terrorist attacks of September 11, 2001. We believe that the military missions in Iraq and Afghanistan have also had a large but difficult-to-measure impact on decisions about technical collection and communications technologies. Going forward, even where a military rationale exists for information collection and use, there increasingly will be countervailing reasons not to see the issue in purely military terms. The convergence of military and civilian communications supports our recommendations for greater civilian control of NSA as well as a separation of NSA from US Cyber Command. It is vital for our intelligence agencies to support our warfighters, but we must develop governance structures attuned to the multiple goals of US policy.

2. Specific Organizational Reforms

***Recommendation 22*:** We recommend that:

(1) the Director of the National Security Agency should be a Senate-confirmed position;
(2) civilians should be eligible to hold that position; and
(3) the President should give serious consideration to making the next Director of the National Security Agency a civilian.

The Director of NSA has not been a Senate-confirmed position; selection has been in the hands of the President alone. Because of the great impact of NSA actions, the need for public confidence in the Director, the value of public trust, and the importance of the traditional system of checks and balances, Senate confirmation is appropriate. Senate confirmation would increase both transparency and accountability.

When appointing the directors of other intelligence organizations, Presidents have exercised their discretion to choose from the ranks of both civilian and military personnel. Both active duty military officers and civilians have been selected to be the Director of the CIA and the Director of the National Reconnaissance (NRO). It is important to the future of NSA that it be understood by the American people to be acting under appropriate controls and supervision.

For this reason, civilians should be eligible for the position. The convergence of civilian and military communications technology makes it increasingly important to have civilian leadership to complement NSA's military and intelligence missions. We believe that the President should seriously consider appointing a civilian to be the next Director of NSA, thus making it clear that NSA operates under civilian control. A senior (two or three-star) military officer should be among the Deputy Directors.

***Recommendation 23*:** We recommend that the National Security Agency should be clearly designated as a foreign intelligence organization; missions other than foreign intelligence collection should generally be reassigned elsewhere.

NSA now has multiple missions and mandates, some of which are blurred, inherently conflicting, or both. Fundamentally, NSA is and should be a foreign intelligence organization. It should not be a domestic security service, a military command, or an information assurance organization. Because of its extraordinary capabilities, effective oversight must exist outside of the Agency.

In some respects, NSA is now both a military and a civilian organization. It has always been led by a military flag rank officer, and its incumbent also serves as the head of a combatant command (US Cyber Command). As matter of history, the evolution in the roles and missions of NSA is understandable; those roles have emerged as a result of a series of historical contingencies and perceived necessities and conveniences. But if the nation were writing on a blank slate, we believe it unlikely that we would create the current organization.

The President should make it clear that NSA's primary mission is the collection of foreign intelligence, including the support of our warfighters. Like other agencies, there are situations in which NSA does and should provide support to the Department of Justice, the Department of Homeland Security, and other law enforcement entities. But it should not assume the lead for programs that are primarily domestic in nature. Missions that do not involve the collection of foreign intelligence should generally be assigned elsewhere.

Recommendation 24: We recommend that the head of the military unit, US Cyber Command, and the Director of the National Security Agency should not be a single official.

As the Pentagon has recognized, it is essential for the United States military to have an effective combatant command for cyberspace activities. The importance of this command will likely grow over time, as specialized cyber capabilities become a growing part of both offense and defense. But the military organization created under Title 10 of the US Code (Defense and military organizations) should be separate from the foreign intelligence agencies created under Title 50 (Intelligence). Just as NSA has provided essential support to US Central Command in the recent wars in Iraq and Afghanistan, NSA should provide intelligence support to US Cyber Command. Nonetheless, there is a pressing need to clarify the distinction between the combat and intelligence collection missions. Standard military doctrine does not place the intelligence function in control of actual combat. Because the two roles are complementary but distinct, the Director of NSA and the Commander of US Cyber Command in the future should not be the same person. Now that Cyber Command has grown past its initial stages, the risk increases that a single commander will not be the best way to achieve the two distinct functions.

Recommendation 25: We recommend that the Information Assurance Directorate—a large component of the National Security Agency that is not engaged in activities related to foreign intelligence—should become a separate agency within the Department of Defense, reporting to the cyber policy element within the Office of the Secretary of Defense.

In keeping with the concept that NSA should be a foreign intelligence agency, the large and important Information Assurance Directorate (IAD) of NSA should be organizationally separate and have a different reporting structure. IAD's primary mission is to ensure the security of the DOD's communications systems. Over time, the importance has grown of its other missions and activities, such as providing support for the security of other US Government networks and making contributions to the overall field of cyber security, including for the vast bulk of US systems that are outside of the government. Those are not missions of a foreign intelligence agency. The historical mission of protecting the military's communications is today a diminishing subset of overall cyber security efforts.

We are concerned that having IAD embedded in a foreign intelligence organization creates potential conflicts of interest. A chief goal of NSA is to access and decrypt SIGINT, an offensive capability. By contrast, IAD's job is defense. When the offensive personnel find some way into a communications device, software system, or network, they may be reluctant to have a patch that blocks their own access. This conflict of interest has been a prominent feature of recent writings by technologists about surveillance issues.[161]

A related concern about keeping IAD in NSA is that there can be an asymmetry within a bureaucracy between offense and defense—a successful offensive effort provides new intelligence that is visible to senior management, while the steady day-to-day efforts on defense offer fewer opportunities for dramatic success.

Another reason to separate IAD from NSA is to foster better relations with the private sector, academic experts, and other cyber security stakeholders. Precisely because so much of cyber security exists in the private sector, including for critical infrastructure, it is vital to maintain public trust. Our discussions with a range of experts have highlighted a current lack of trust that NSA is committed to the defensive mission. Creating a new organizational structure would help rebuild that trust going forward.

There are, of course, strong technical reasons for information-sharing between the offense and defense for cyber security. Individual experts learn by having experience both in penetrating systems and in seeking to block penetration. Such collaboration could and must occur even if IAD is organizationally separate.

In an ideal world, IAD could form the core of the cyber capability of DHS. DHS has been designated as the lead cabinet department for cyber security defense. Any effort to transfer IAD out of the Defense Department budget, however, would likely meet with opposition in Congress.[162] Thus, we suggest that IAD should become a Defense Agency, with status similar to that of the Defense Information Systems Agency (DISA) or the Defense Threat Reduction Agency (DTRA). Under this approach, the new and separate Defense Information Assurance Agency (DIAA) would no longer report through intelligence channels, but would be subject to oversight by the cyber security policy arm of the Office of the Secretary of Defense.

C. Reforming Organizations Dedicated to the Protection of Privacy and Civil Liberties

The Executive Branch should adopt structural reforms to protect privacy and civil liberties in connection with intelligence collection and the use of personal information. Specifically, the Executive Branch should improve its policies and procedures in the realms of policy clearance and development, compliance, oversight and investigations, and technology assessment.

A fundamental theme of this Report is that the fact that the intelligence community is able to collect personal information does not mean that it should do so. Similarly, the fact that collection is legal does not mean that it is good policy. The Intelligence Community's ability to collect and use information has expanded exponentially with the increased use of electronic communications technologies. The priority placed on national security after the attacks of September 11, including large budget increases, has made possible an enormous range of new collection and sharing capabilities, both within and outside the United States, on scales greater than previously imagined.

With this expansion of capabilities, there should be an accompanying set of institutions, properly funded, to ensure that the overall national interest is achieved in connection with intelligence collection and use. We recommend institutional changes within the Executive

Branch designed to strengthen (1) policy clearance and development; (2) compliance; (3) oversight; and (4) technology assessment.

***Recommendation 26*:** We recommend the creation of a privacy and civil liberties policy official located both in the National Security Staff and the Office of Management and Budget.

In some recent periods, the NSS, reporting in the White House to the President's National Security Advisor, has had a civil servant tasked with privacy issues. During that time, the Office of Management and Budget (OMB), which in its management role oversees privacy and cyber security, has similarly had a civil servant with privacy responsibilities. We recommend that the President name a policy official, who would sit within both the NSS and the OMB, to coordinate US Government policy on privacy, including issues within the Intelligence Community.

This position would resemble in some respects the position of Chief Counselor for Privacy in OMB under President Clinton, from 1999 until early 2001. There are several reasons for creating this position: First, the OMB-run clearance process is an efficient and effective way to ensure that privacy issues are considered by policymakers. Second, a political appointee is more likely to be effective than a civil servant. Third, identifying a single, publicly named official provides a focal point for outside experts, advocacy groups, industry, foreign governments, and others to inform the policy process. Fourth, this policy development role is distinct from that of ensuring compliance by the agencies.[163]

***Recommendation 27*:** We recommend that:

(1) The charter of the Privacy and Civil Liberties Oversight Board should be modified to create a new and strengthened agency, the Civil Liberties and Privacy Protection Board, that can oversee Intelligence Community activities for foreign intelligence purposes, rather than only for counterterrorism purposes;
(2) The Civil Liberties and Privacy Protection Board should be an authorized recipient for whistle-blower complaints related to privacy and civil liberties concerns from employees in the Intelligence Community;
(3) An Office of Technology Assessment should be created within the Civil Liberties and Privacy Protection Board to assess Intelligence Community technology initiatives and support privacy-enhancing technologies; and
(4) Some compliance functions, similar to outside auditor functions in corporations, should be shifted from the National Security Agency and perhaps other intelligence agencies to the Civil Liberties and Privacy Protection Board.

1. ***Creating the CLPP Board.*** The 9/11 Commission recommended creation of what is now the PCLOB, an independent agency in the Executive Branch designed to conduct oversight of Intelligence Community activities related to terrorism and to make recommendations to Congress and the Executive Branch about how to improve privacy and civil liberty protections. The statute that authorizes the PCLOB gives it jurisdiction only over information collected and used for anti-terrorism purposes. There are major privacy and civil liberties issued raised by Intelligence Community collections for other foreign intelligence purposes, including anti-proliferation, counter-intelligence, economic policy, and other foreign affairs purposes.

To match the scope of information collection and use, we recommend the creation of a new and strengthened Board that has authority to oversee the full range of foreign intelligence issues. We have considered whether changes should be made to the existing PCLOB, or whether instead it would be better to create an entirely new agency with augmented powers. An advantage of keeping the PCLOB as the organizational base is that a Chair and four Board members have already been confirmed by the Senate and are in place. On the other hand, the scope of responsibility that we contemplate for the agency is considerably broader than the existing PCLOB statute permits. There are also flaws with the current PCLOB statute. For those reasons, we recommend creation of a new independent agency in the Executive Branch. We refer to this new agency as the Civil Liberties and Privacy Protection Board, or CLPP Board.

Oversight should match the scope of the activity being reviewed. Having the new CLPP Board oversee "foreign intelligence" rather than "anti-terrorism" would match the scope of FISA. This broader scope would reduce any temptation Intelligence Community agencies might have to mischaracterize their activities as something other than anti-terrorism in order to avoid review by the current PCLOB.

We anticipate that this expanded scope would call for substantially increased funding and staff. With its current small staff, the PCLOB is limited in its ability to oversee intelligence agencies operating on the scale of tens of billions of dollars. This must be addressed. As with the PCLOB, the CLPP Board leadership and staff should have the clearances required to oversee this broader range of Intelligence Community activities. As under current statutes, the CLPP Board would make regular reports to Congress and the public, in a suitable mix of classified and unclassified forms.

2. ***The CLPP Board and Whistle-blowers.*** We recommend enactment of a statute that creates a path for whistle-blowers to report their concerns directly to the CLPP Board. Various criticisms have been published about the effectiveness of current whistle-blower provisions in the Intelligence Community. Although we have not evaluated all of these criticisms, the oversight and investigations role of the CLPP Board is well matched to examining whistle-blower allegations.

3. ***A CLPP Board Office of Technology Assessment.*** Public policy is shaped in part by what is technically possible, and technology experts are essential to analyzing the range of the possible. An improved technology assessment function is essential to informing policymakers about the range of options, both for collection and use of personal information, and also about the cost and effectiveness of privacy-enhancing technologies.

Prior to 1995, Congress had an Office of Technology Assessment that did significant studies on privacy and related issues. The OTA was then abolished, and no similar federal agency has existed since. Because the effectiveness of privacy and civil liberties protections depend heavily on the information technology used, a steady stream of new privacy and technology issues faces the Intelligence Community. For instance, the last few years have seen explosive growth in social networking, cloud computing, and Big Data analytics. Because the Intelligence Community pushes the state of the art to achieve military and other foreign policy objectives, assessment of the technological changes must be up-to-date.

We therefore recommend that the government should have an Office of Technology Assessment that does not report directly to the Intelligence Community but that has access to

Intelligence Community activities. Congress is vital to oversight of the Intelligence Community, but it does not have an office to enable it to assess technological developments. The CLPP Board, with classified personnel and agency independence, is the logical place for this sort of independent assessment.

4. ***Compliance Activities.*** Although the Compliance program at NSA is independent and professional, there may be a public impression that any internal oversight function, at any agency, is vulnerable to pressure from the agency's leadership. To increase public trust and overcome even the perception of agency bias in NSA Compliance program, some of the compliance function and the relevant staff should be transferred to the CLPP Board. This structure would be analogous to the complementary roles of internal and external auditors familiar in public corporations. Under this approach, NSA would retain the internal compliance function, with the external function shifting to the CLPP Board. Consideration should also be given to transferring elements of other agencies' compliance functions to the CLPP Board.

5. ***Technical Amendments to PCLOB Statute.*** The current PCLOB statute has a number of limitations that reduce its ability to operate effectively. If a new CLPP Board is not created, we recommend that several changes be made to the PCLOB statute. First, the four members of the Board other than the Chair are unpaid government employees who are permitted to work only a limited number of days per year on PCLOB matters. We recommend that these Board members should be paid for their service, and that they should not be restricted in the amount of service they provide in a year. Second, the current statute suggests that only the Chair can hire staff; any vacancy in the Chair position thus creates uncertainty about the legal basis for staff hiring. The statute should be amended to ensure smooth functioning of the Board even if the Chair position is vacant. Third, the Board should have the ability, held by other federal agencies, to subpoena records held in the private sector, without the current prior review of subpoena requests by the Attorney General. Fourth, the PCLOB needs better institutional assistance from the Intelligence Community to ensure administrative support for the Board's efforts. For instance, Board members sometimes need access to a classified facility outside of the Washington, DC headquarters, and ODNI or other support would make it easier to gain that access.

D. Reforming the FISA Court

***Recommendation 28*:** We recommend that:

(1) Congress should create the position of Public Interest Advocate to represent privacy and civil liberties interests before the Foreign Intelligence Surveillance Court;
(2) the Foreign Intelligence Surveillance Court should have greater technological expertise available to the judges;
(3) the transparency of the Foreign Intelligence Surveillance Court's decisions should be increased, including by instituting declassification reviews that comply with existing standards; and

(4) Congress should change the process by which judges are appointed to the Foreign Intelligence Surveillance Court, with the appointment power divided among the Supreme Court Justices.

As we have seen, the FISC was established by the Foreign Intelligence Surveillance Act of 1978. The FISC, which today consists of eleven federal district court judges serving staggered seven-year terms, was created as a result of recommendations of the Church Committee to enable judicial oversight of classified foreign intelligence investigations. Most often, the judges of the FISC rule on government applications for the issuance of (a) FISA warrants authorizing electronic surveillance, (b) orders for section 215 business records, and (c) orders for section 702 interceptions targeting non-United States persons who are outside the United States.

The FISC has a staff of five full-time legal assistants with expertise in foreign intelligence issues. When preparing to rule on applications for such orders, the FISC's legal assistants often deal directly with the government's attorneys. Sometimes the judge approves the application without a hearing, and sometimes the judge concludes that a hearing with the government's attorneys is appropriate. FISA does not provide a mechanism for the FISC to invite the views of nongovernmental parties. Rather, the FISC's proceedings are *ex parte*, as required by statute, and consistent with the procedures followed by other federal courts in ruling on applications for search warrants and wiretap orders.[164]

Critics of the FISC have noted that the court grants more than 99 percent of all requested applications. In a recent letter to the Chairman of the Senate Judiciary Committee, FISC Presiding Judge Reggie Walton explained that this statistic is misleading, because that figure does "not reflect the fact that many applications are altered prior to final submission or even withheld from final submission entirely, often after an indication that a judge would not approve them."[165] Judge Walton's explanation seems quite credible. Moreover, this understanding of the FISC's approach is reinforced by the FISC's strong record in dealing with non-compliance issues when they are brought to its attention. As illustrated by the section 215 and section 702 non-compliance incidents discussed in sections III and IV of this Report, the FISC takes seriously its responsibility to hold the government accountable for its errors.

We believe that reform of the FISC in the following areas will strengthen its ability to serve the national security interests of the United States while protecting privacy and civil liberties and promoting greater transparency.

(a) ***Establishing a Public Interest Advocate.*** Our legal tradition is committed to the adversary system. When the government initiates a proceeding against a person, that person is usually entitled to representation by an advocate who is committed to protecting her interests. If it is functioning well, the adversary system is an engine of truth. It is built on the assumption that judges are in a better position to find the right answer on questions of law and fact when they hear competing views.

When the FISC was created, it was assumed that it would resolve routine and individualized questions of fact, akin to those involved when the government seeks a search warrant. It was not anticipated that the FISC would address the kinds of questions that benefit from, or require, an adversary presentation. When the government applies for a warrant, it must establish "probable cause," but an adversary proceeding is not involved. As both technology and the law have evolved over time, however, the FISC is sometimes presented with novel and complex issues of law. The resolution of such issues would benefit from an adversary proceeding.

A good example is the question whether section 215 authorized the bulk telephony meta-data program. That question posed serious and difficult questions of statutory and constitutional interpretation about which reasonable lawyers and judges could certainly differ. On such a question, an adversary presentation of the competing arguments is likely to result in a better decision. Hearing only the government's side of the question leaves the judge without a researched and informed presentation of an opposing view.

We recommend that Congress should create a Public Interest Advocate, who would have the authority to intervene in matters that raise such issues. The central task of the Public Interest Advocate would be to represent the interests of those whose rights of privacy or civil liberties might be at stake. The Advocate might be invited to participate by a FISC judge. In addition, and because a judge might not always appreciate the importance of an adversary proceeding in advance, we recommend that the Advocate should receive docketing information about applications to the FISC, enabling her to intervene on her own initiative (that is, without an invitation from a FISC judge).

One difficult issue is where the Advocate should be housed. Because the number of FISA applications that raise novel or contentious issues is probably small, the Advocate might find herself with relatively little to do. It might therefore be sensible for the Advocate to have other responsibilities. One possibility would be for the Public Advocate to be on the staff of the CLPP Board, thus giving her other responsibilities and providing knowledge about the workings of the intelligence agencies. A drawback of this approach is that the Board has multiple roles, and it is possible that the presence of the Public Advocate in that setting might create conflicts of interest. Another possibility is to outsource the Public Advocate responsibility either to a law firm or a public interest group for a sufficiently long period that its lawyers could obtain the necessary clearances and have continuity of knowledge about the intelligence agencies.[166] Under the former approach, the Advocate would be designated by the CLPP Board from among its employees; under the latter, the CLPP Board could oversee a procurement process to appoint the outside group of lawyers.

(b) ***Bolster Technological Capacity***. The recently published opinions of the FISC make evident the technological complexity of many of the issues that now come before it. The compliance issues involving section 215 and 702 illustrate this reality and the extent to which it is important for the FISC to have the expertise available to it to oversee such issues.

Rather than relying predominantly on staff lawyers in its efforts to address these matters, the FISC should be able to call on independent technologists, with appropriate clearances, who do not report to NSA or Department of Justice. One approach would be for the FISC to use the court-appointed experts; another would be for the FISC to draw upon technologists who work with the CLPP Board.

(c) ***Transparency.*** The US Government should re-examine the process by which decisions issued by the FISC and its appellate body, the Foreign Intelligence Surveillance Court of Review (FISC-R) are reviewed for declassification and determine whether it ought to implement a more robust and regimented process of declassification of decisions to improve transparency.

The majority of the FISC's orders and filings are classified "Secret" or "Top Secret" using the standards set forth in Section 1 of Executive Order 13526 issued by President Obama on December 29, 2009. Under this Executive Order, classified national security information is subject to automatic declassification review upon passage of 25 years.

Pursuant to the Department of Justice's Automatic Classification Guide dated November 2012, "FISA Files"[167] are exempted from automatic declassification review at 25 years under a "File Series Exemption" granted by the Assistant to the President for National Security Affairs on October 5, 2006. These records are not subject to automatic declassification review until they reach 50 years in age from the date they were created. Consequently, the public is left uninformed as to decisions that may have far-reaching implications in terms of how the FISC interpreted the law.

The very idea of the rule of law requires a high degree of transparency. Transparency promotes accountability. As Justice Louis Brandeis once observed, sunlight can be "the best of disinfectants."[168] A lack of transparency can also breed confusion, suspicion, and distrust. In our system, judicial proceedings are generally open to the public, and judicial opinions are made available for public scrutiny and inspection. Indeed, the ODNI has declassified a considerable number of FISC opinions in 2013, making the determination that the gains from transparency outweighed the risk to national security.

There can, of course, be a genuine need for confidentiality, especially when classified material is involved. When the FISC is dealing with such material, there are legitimate limits on disclosure. But in order to further the rule of law, FISC opinions or, when appropriate, redacted versions of FISC opinions, should be made public in a timely manner, unless secrecy of the opinion is essential to the effectiveness of a properly classified program.

(d) ***Selection and Composition of the FISC.*** Under FISA, the judges on the FISC are selected by the Chief Justice of the United States. In theory, this method of selection has significant advantages. Concentration of the power of appointment in one person can make the process more orderly and organized. But that approach has drawn two legitimate criticisms.

The first involves the potential risks associated with giving a single person, even the Chief Justice, the authority to select *all* of the members of an important court. The second involves the fact that ten of the eleven current FISC judges, all of whom were appointed by the current Chief Justice, were appointed to the federal bench by Republican presidents. Although the role of a judge is to follow the law and not to make political judgments, Republican-appointed and Democratic-appointed judges sometimes have divergent views, including on issues involving privacy, civil liberties, and claims of national security. There is therefore a legitimate reason for concern if, as is now the case, the judges on the FISC turn out to come disproportionately from either Republican or Democratic appointees.

There are several ways to respond to this concern. We recommend allocating the appointment authority to the Circuit Justices. Under this approach, each member of the Supreme Court would have the authority to select one or two members of the FISC from within the Circuit(s) over which she or he has jurisdiction. This approach would have the advantage of dividing appointment authority among the Court's nine members and reducing the risks associated with concentrating the appointment power in a single person.

SECTION VII. GLOBAL COMMUNICATIONS TECHNOLOGY: PROMOTING PROSPERITY, SECURITY, AND OPENNESS IN A NETWORKED WORLD

A. Introduction

An important goal of US policy is to promote prosperity, security, and openness in the predominant method of modern communication, the Internet. This section examines how to achieve that goal, consistent with other goals of US policy.

In 2011, the Obama Administration released a major report: "International Strategy for Cyberspace: Prosperity, Security, and Openness in a Networked World." In the letter introducing the report, President Obama wrote: "This strategy outlines not only a vision for the future of cyberspace, but an agenda for realizing it. It provides the context for our partners at home and abroad to understand our priorities, and how we can come together to preserve the character of cyberspace and reduce the threats we face."

The Strategy defined the overall goal: "The United States will work internationally to promote an **open, interoperable, secure, and reliable** information and communications infrastructure that supports international trade and commerce, strengthens international security, and fosters free expression and innovation" (emphasis added).

We believe that this is an exceedingly important goal, and that it bears directly on efforts to engage in sensible risk management.

In this section, we offer a series of recommendations designed to promote that goal, and in the process to protect the central values associated with a free Internet.

B. Background: Trade, Internet Freedom, and Other Goals

The United States has a strong interest in promoting an open, interoperable, secure, and reliable information and communication structure. We focus our discussion on international trade, economic growth, and Internet freedom.

Throughout this report, we have stressed the need for a risk- management approach, balancing the imperatives for intelligence collection with the potential downsides. In the areas discussed in this section, prominent US policy goals run the risk of being undermined by the reports about US surveillance.

We consider what measures will best achieve those goals for our global communications structure.

1. International Trade and Economic Growth

The US is committed to international economic competitiveness, to improvements in the international trade system, and to achievement of economic growth. The rules for international trade are crucial for the pervasively international conduct of commerce on the Internet, as well as for other sectors involved in international trade. Free trade agreements can contribute to economic growth. Unfortunately, foreign concerns about US surveillance threaten achievement of these various goals.

For example, the Transatlantic Trade and Investment Partnership (T- TIP) is a large and visible trade negotiation potentially affected by the recent surveillance leaks. The T-TIP talks were launched in 2013 as "an ambitious, comprehensive, and high-standard trade and investment agreement" designed to eliminate all tariffs on trade, improve market access on trade in services, and address a wide range of other impediments to trade.[169] But strong concerns have been expressed about surveillance by European officials, as reflected in this statement by the EU Parliament Committee on Foreign Affairs: "With the damage to trust in the transatlantic relationship caused by NSA massive surveillance and lack of data privacy remedies for Europeans, the transatlantic economic relationship is at risk." [170]

European officials have similarly expressed doubt about whether to continue the existing Safe Harbor agreement for transfer of personal information to the US, under which companies are able to comply with the stricter EU privacy laws.[171] Although the precise impact on such future negotiations is unclear, such statements show the linkage between intelligence collection decisions and international trade negotiations.

The effects of concern with US surveillance on US trade in cloud computing and other online activities have drawn particular attention. The public cloud computing market for enterprises is growing rapidly. By 2016, it is estimated to reach $207 billion annually, more than double the 2012 level.[172]

As a result, cloud computing vendors not only have to retain existing customers but also must recruit new customers to maintain market share. In the wake of press reports on US surveillance, two studies estimated large losses in sales for US cloud computing providers, due to concerns overseas about the security of US providers and possible legal measures to limit use of US-based cloud providers by other countries. [173] US-based information technology companies and trade associations have expressed strong concerns, fearing that Chinese, European, and other competitors will use the disclosures to promote their products over American exports.

Negative effects stemming from concern with US surveillance on trade and economic competitiveness may, in turn, have adverse effects on overall US economic growth. In recent years, the information technology sector has been a major source of innovation and growth. Foreign concerns about US surveillance can directly reduce the market share of US-based technology companies, and can in addition have an indirect effect of justifying protectionist measures. Addressing concerns about US Government surveillance would increase confidence in the US information technology sector, thus contributing to US economic growth.

2. Internet Freedom

US Internet freedom policy seeks to preserve and expand the Internet as an open, global space for free expression, for organizing and interaction, and for commerce. In recent years, the United States has highlighted Internet freedom as an important goal of US policy, including by pushing successfully in 2012 for the first United Nations resolution that confirms that human rights in the Internet realm must be protected with the same commitment as in the real world.

The US has worked with the Dutch Foreign Ministry to establish the Freedom Online Coalition, currently a group of 21 governments from five regions committed to coordinating diplomatic efforts to advance Internet freedom. This Coalition has sought to broaden support for an approach based on universal human rights and the inclusive, multi-stakeholder model of Internet governance.

A central theme of US Internet freedom policy has been protection against intrusive surveillance and repression. The US Government has consistently spoken out against the arrest and persecution of bloggers and online activists in countries such as Azerbaijan, China, Cuba, Egypt, Ethiopia, Iran, Russia, Saudi Arabia, Thailand, Venezuela, and Vietnam. President Obama and Secretaries of State have publicly criticized restrictive Internet legislation designed to force companies to collaborate in censorship and pervasive surveillance of their users in order to chill expression and facilitate persecution. Since 2008, the Department of State and the United States Agency for International Development have invested over $100 million in programs to enable human rights activists and bloggers to exercise their human rights freely and safely online, including by distribution of strong encryption and other anti-censorship tools.

Revelations about US surveillance have threatened to undermine the US Internet freedom agenda. Countries that were previously criticized by the United States for excessive surveillance have accused the US of hypocrisy. In our view, these allegations lack force. US surveillance is subject to oversight by the multiple authorities shown in Appendix C, and the First Amendment protections under the US Constitution are an effective bulwark against censorship and political repression.

Nonetheless, the reports about US surveillance have clearly made it more difficult to explain the key differences in international fora. As we have emphasized at several points in this Report, public trust is exceedingly important.

3. Internet Governance and Localization Requirements

The United States has strongly supported an inclusive multi- stakeholder model of Internet governance in order to maintain and expand a globally interoperable, open, and secure Internet architecture to which all people have access. This multi-stakeholder approach incorporates input from industry, governments, civil society, academic institutions, technical experts, and others. This approach has emphasized the primacy of interoperable and secure technical standards, selected with the help of technical experts.

A competing model, favored by Russia and a number of other countries, would place Internet governance under the auspices of the United Nations and the International Telecommunications Union (ITU).

This model would enhance the influence of governments at the expense of other stakeholders in Internet governance decisions, and it could legitimize greater state control over Internet content and communications. In particular, this model could support greater use of "localization" requirements, such as national laws requiring servers to be physically located within a country or limits on transferring data across borders.

The press revelations about US surveillance have emboldened supporters of localization requirements for Internet communications.

Brazil, Indonesia, and Vietnam have proposed requiring e-mails and other Internet communications to be stored locally, in the particular country. Although generally favoring the multi-stakeholder approach to many Internet governance issues, the EU has also shifted in the direction of localization requirements.

In the second half of 2013, the EU Parliament voted in favor of a proposal to limit international data flows; this provision would prohibit responding to lawful government requests, including from the US courts and government, until release of such records were approved by a European data protection authority.

Public debate has suggested a possible mix of motives supporting such localization requirements, including (1) concern about how records about their citizens will be treated in the US; (2) support for local cloud providers and other information technology companies with the effect of reducing the market share of US providers; and (3) use of the localization proposals as a way to highlight concerns about US intelligence practices and create leverage for possible changes in US policy. Whatever the mix of motives, press reports about US surveillance have posed new challenges for the longstanding US policy favoring the multi-stakeholder approach to Internet governance as well as US opposition to localization requirements.

C. Technical Measures to Increase Security and User Confidence

***Recommendation 29*:** We recommend that, regarding encryption, the US Government should:

(1) fully support and not undermine efforts to create encryption standards;
(2) not in any way subvert, undermine, weaken, or make vulnerable generally available commercial software; and
(3) increase the use of encryption and urge US companies to do so, in order to better protect data in transit, at rest, in the cloud, and in other storage.

Encryption is an essential basis for trust on the Internet; without such trust, valuable communications would not be possible. For the entire system to work, encryption software itself must be trustworthy. Users of encryption must be confident, and justifiably confident, that only those people they designate can decrypt their data.

The use of reliable encryption software to safeguard data is critical to many sectors and organizations, including financial services, medicine and health care, research and development, and other critical infrastructures in the United States and around the world. Encryption allows users of information technology systems to trust that their data, including their financial transactions, will not be altered or stolen. Encryption-related software, including pervasive examples such as Secure Sockets Layer (SSL) and Public Key Infrastructure (PKI), is essential to online commerce and user authentication. It is part of the underpinning of current communications networks. Indeed, in light of the massive increase in cyber-crime and intellectual property theft on-line, the use of encryption should be greatly expanded to protect not only data in transit, but also data at rest on networks, in storage, and in the cloud.

We are aware of recent allegations that the United States Government has intentionally introduced "backdoors" into commercially available software, enabling decryption of apparently secure software. We are also aware that some people have expressed concern that such "backdoors" could be discovered and used by criminal cartels and other governments, and hence that some commercially available software is not trustworthy today.

Upon review, however, we are unaware of any vulnerability created by the US Government in generally available commercial software that puts users at risk of criminal hackers or foreign governments decrypting their data. Moreover, it appears that in the vast majority of generally used, commercially available encryption software, there is no vulnerability, or "backdoor," that makes it possible for the US Government or anyone else to achieve unauthorized access.[174]

Nonetheless, it is important to take strong steps to enhance trust in this basic underpinning of information technology. Recommendation 32 is designed to describe those steps. The central point is that trust in encryption standards, and in the resulting software, must be maintained. Although NSA has made clear that it has not and is not now doing the activities listed below, the US Government should make it clear that:

- NSA will not engineer vulnerabilities into the encryption algorithms that guard global commerce;
- The United States will not provide competitive advantage to US firms by the provision to those corporations of industrial espionage;
- NSA will not demand changes in any product by any vendor for the purpose of undermining the security or integrity of the product, or to ease NSA's clandestine collection of information by users of the product; and
- NSA will not hold encrypted communication as a way to avoid retention limits.

Although NSA is authorized to retain encrypted data indefinitely for cryptanalysis purposes, such as for encryption systems of nation-states or terrorist groups, NSA should not store generic commercial encrypted data, such as Virtual Private Network (VPN) or SSL data. If NSA is able to decrypt data years after it is collected, that data, once decrypted, should be sent to an analytic storage facility, where standard retention, minimization, and reporting rules would apply. Those rules should include minimization of US person data and a prohibition on using data that is beyond authorized retention limits.

Recommendation 30**:** We recommend that the National Security Council staff should manage an interagency process to review on a regular basis the activities of the US Government regarding attacks that exploit a previously unknown vulnerability in a computer application or system. These are often called "Zero Day" attacks because developers have had zero days to address and patch the vulnerability. US policy should generally move to ensure that Zero Days are quickly blocked, so that the underlying vulnerabilities are patched on US Government and other networks. In rare instances, US policy may briefly authorize using a Zero Day for high priority intelligence collection, following senior, interagency review involving all appropriate departments.

NSA and other US Government agencies, such as DHS, have important missions to assist US corporations in the protection of privately owned and operated critical infrastructure information networks.

To do so, NSA, DHS, and other agencies should identify vulnerabilities in software widely employed in critical infrastructure and then work to eliminate those vulnerabilities as quickly as possible. That duty to defend, however, may sometimes come into conflict with the intelligence collection mission, particularly when it comes to what are known as "Zero Days."

A Zero Day or "0 Day" exploit is a previously unknown vulnerability in software in a computer application or system – the developers or system owners have had zero days to address or patch the vulnerability. Because the software attack technique has not been used or seen before, it enables a cyber attacker to penetrate a system or to achieve other malicious goals. In almost all instances, for widely used code, it is in the national interest to eliminate software vulnerabilities rather than to use them for US intelligence collection. Eliminating the vulnerabilities—"patching" them— strengthens the security of US Government, critical infrastructure, and other computer systems.

We recommend that, when an urgent and significant national security priority can be addressed by the use of a Zero Day, an agency of the US Government may be authorized to use temporarily a Zero Day instead of immediately fixing the underlying vulnerability. Before approving use of the Zero Day rather than patching a vulnerability, there should be a senior-level, interagency approval process that employs a risk management approach. The NSS should chair the process, with regular reviews. All offices and departments with relevant concerns, generally including the National Economic Council, State, Commerce, Energy, and Homeland Security, should be involved in that process.

D. Institutional Measures for Cyberspace

***Recommendation 31*:** We recommend that the United States should support international norms or international agreements for specific measures that will increase confidence in the security of online communications. Among those measures to be considered are:

(1) Governments should not use surveillance to steal industry secrets to advantage their domestic industry;
(2) Governments should not use their offensive cyber capabilities to change the amounts held in financial accounts or otherwise manipulate the financial systems;
(3) Governments should promote transparency about the number and type of law enforcement and other requests made to communications providers;
(4) Absent a specific and compelling reason, governments should avoid localization requirements that (a) mandate location of servers and other information technology facilities or (b) prevent trans-border data flows.

The US Government should encourage other countries to take specific measures to limit the possible negative consequences of their own intelligence activities, and increase public trust and user confidence in the security of online communications. Norms or agreements might be valuable for that purpose.

We suggest consideration of a series of specific steps. First, governments should not use their surveillance capabilities to steal industry secrets to advantage their domestic industries. Surveillance may take place against both foreign and domestic companies for a variety of reasons, such as to promote compliance with anti-money laundering, anti-corruption, and other laws, as well as international agreements such as economic sanctions against certain countries. The purpose of such surveillance, however, should not be to enable a government to favor its domestic industry. Bolstering an international norm against this sort of economic espionage and competition would support economic growth, protect investment and innovation in intellectual property, and reduce costs to those innovators of protecting against nation-state cyber attacks.

Second, governments should abstain from penetrating the systems of financial institutions and changing the amounts held in accounts there. The policy of avoiding tampering with account balances in financial institutions is part of a broader US policy of abstaining from manipulation of the financial system. These policies support economic growth by allowing all actors to rely on the accuracy of financial statements without the need for costly re-verification of account balances. This sort of attack could cause damaging uncertainty in financial markets, as well as create a risk of escalating counter-attacks against a nation that began such an effort. The US Government should affirm this policy as an international norm, and incorporate the policy into free trade or other international agreements.

Third, governments should increase transparency about requests in other countries from communications providers. Elsewhere in this Report, we discuss the importance of such transparency, and recommend increasing reporting by both providers and the US Government. Transparency about the number and nature of such requests serves as a check against abuse of the lawful access process. Greater transparency can also encourage increased trust in the security of Internet communications and reduce the risk that governments are obtaining widespread access to private communication records without the knowledge of users. Putting this sort of provision into free trade agreements or other international instruments can broaden the positive effects of greater transparency within the US.

Fourth, we support international efforts to limit localization requirements except where there is a specific and compelling reason for such actions. Global inter-operability has been a fundamental technical feature of the Internet; bits flow from one user to the next based on technical considerations rather than national boundaries. National efforts to tamper with this architecture would require pervasive technical changes and be costly in economic terms. A balkanized Internet, sometimes referred to as a "splinternet," would greatly reduce the economic, political, cultural, and other benefits of modern communications technologies. The US Government should work with allies to reduce harmful efforts to impose localization rules onto the Internet.

Recommendation 32: We recommend that there be an Assistant Secretary of State to lead diplomacy of international information technology issues.

In the wake of recent disclosures, distortions, and controversies involving US Government intelligence collection, there is an increased need for vigorous, coordinated, senior-level US diplomacy across a broad range of inter-related information technology issues. We believe that the US should take the lead in proposing an agreement among multiple nations to some set of Internet Norms for Cyberspace, such as a prohibition on industrial espionage, a protection of financial services and markets data standard, and others. To this end, we recommend a US diplomatic agenda to promote confidence-building measures for international cyber security, building on the Budapest Convention on Cyber Crime. The promotion of the Internet Freedom Agenda, the protection of intellectual property rights in cyber space, changes in Internet governance and the implementation of the President's International Cyber Strategy—all will necessitate agile diplomatic activity by the United States.

Currently, there is no single, senior US diplomat and no single Department of State Bureau, with lead responsibility across this broad set of issues. Just as other international, non-regional functional issues have in the past benefited from the creation of an Assistant Secretary of State position and of a State Department bureau (International Narcotics,

Environmental Affairs, Counterterrorism, Human Rights), the interests of the United States would be served by the creation of a Department of State Bureau of Internet and Cyberspace Affairs, led by an experienced senior diplomat confirmed by the Senate as an Assistant Secretary of State. The Assistant Secretary would coordinate activity of the regional and functional bureaus on these issues and should, with NSS support, coordinate interagency activities with other governments.

***Recommendation 33*:** We recommend that as part of its diplomatic agenda on international information technology issues, the United States should advocate for, and explain its rationale for, a model of Internet governance that is inclusive of all appropriate stakeholders, not just governments.

The United States Government should continue and strengthen its international advocacy for an Internet governance model that is inclusive of all appropriate stakeholders, not just governments. This recommendation builds on the administration's 2011 International Strategy for Cyberspace, which outlines multiple US Government goals with respect to global communications technologies. It articulates the need to protect national security, while also highlighting the importance of economic growth, openness, privacy protection, and a secure communications infrastructure. Other administration initiatives similarly emphasize the importance of multiple policy goals for online communications, such as the efforts led by the Department of State on the Internet Freedom agenda and the efforts led by the Department of Commerce on the Consumer Privacy Bill of Rights.

As part of the overall discussion of US policy concerning communications technology, we believe that the US Government should reaffirm that Internet governance must not be limited to governments, but should include all appropriate stakeholders. Inclusion of such stakeholders—including civil society, industry, and technical experts—is important to ensure that the process benefits from a wide range of information and to reduce the risk of bias or partiality.

We are aware that some changes in governance approaches may well be desirable to reflect changing communications practices. For instance, the time may well be approaching for a hard look at the unique US relationship to the organization that governs the domain name system, the Internet Corporation for Assigned Names and Numbers (ICANN). The current US role is an artifact of the early history of the Internet, and may not be well suited to the broader set of stakeholders engaged in Internet governance today. The US Government and its allies, however, should continue to oppose shifting governance of the Internet to a forum, such as the International Telecommunications Union, where nation-states dominate the process, often to the exclusion of others. We believe that such a governance shift would threaten the prosperity, security, and openness of online communications.

***Recommendation 34*:** We recommend that the US Government should streamline the process for lawful international requests to obtain electronic communications through the Mutual Legal Assistance Treaty process.

US efforts to obtain improved international cooperation on information technology issues of importance to us are undermined by the inability of the Department of Justice to provide adequate support to other nations when they request our assistance in dealing with cyber crime originating in the United States. The Justice Department has severely under-resourced the so-called Mutual Legal Assistance Treaty (MLAT) support process.

The MLAT process essentially permits one country to seek electronic communication and other records held in other countries. For instance, non-US countries may seek e-mails held in the United States by web e-mail providers. Under the Electronic Communications Privacy Act, providers in the US can turn over the content of e-mails only through the required legal process, typically requiring probable cause that a crime has been committed.

The MLAT process creates a legal mechanism for non-US countries to obtain e-mail records, but the process today is too slow and cumbersome. Requests appear to average approximately 10 months to fulfill, with some requests taking considerably longer. Non-US governments seeking such records can face a frustrating delay in conducting legitimate investigations. These delays provide a rationale for new laws that require e-mail and other records to be held in the other country, thus contributing to the harmful trend of localization laws discussed above.

We believe that the MLAT process in the US should be streamlined, both in order to respond more promptly to legitimate foreign requests and to demonstrate the US commitment to a well-functioning Internet that meets the goals of the international community. Promising reform measures could include:

1. ***Increase resources to the office in the Department of Justice that handles MLAT requests.*** The Office of International Affairs (OIA) in the Department of Justice has had flat or reduced funding over time, despite the large increase in the international electronic communications that are the subject of most MLAT requests.
2. ***Create an online submission form for MLATs.*** Today, there is no online form for foreign governments that seek to use the MLAT process. An online submission process, accompanied by clear information to foreign governments about the MLAT requirements, would make it easier for distant and diverse foreign governments to understand what is required under the US probable cause standard or other laws.
3. ***Streamline the number of steps in the process.*** Under the current system, the OIA first examines a request, and then forwards it to the US Attorney in the district where the records are held. That US Attorney's office then reviews the application a second time, and handles the request subject to the other priorities of that office. The Department of Justice should explore whether a single point of contact would be able to expedite the MLAT request.
4. ***Streamline provision of the records back to the foreign country.*** Under the current system, the provider sends the records to the Department of Justice, which then forwards the records to the requesting country. It may be possible to streamline this process by permitting the provider to send the records directly to the requesting country, with notice to the Justice Department of what has been sent.
5. ***Promote the use of MLATs globally and demonstrate the US Government's commitment to an effective process.*** Changing technology has sharply increased the importance for non-US governments of gaining lawful access to records held in the United States. Web e-mail providers are largely headquartered in the United States, and today's use of secure encryption for e-mail means that other governments frequently cannot intercept and read the e-mail between the user and the server. It is in the interest of the United States to support the continued use of efficient and innovative technologies on the Internet, including through leading web e- mail providers. The US Government can promote this interest by publicizing and

supporting the existence of a well-functioning MLAT process, thereby reducing the likelihood of harmful localization measures.

E. Addressing Future Technological Challenges

This section has thus far addressed issues that are currently known to implicate US intelligence and communications technology policy. Communications technology will continue to change rapidly, however, so institutional mechanisms should be in place to address such changes.

***Recommendation 35*:** We recommend that for big data and data-mining programs directed at communications, the US Government should develop Privacy and Civil Liberties Impact Assessments to ensure that such efforts are statistically reliable, cost-effective, and protective of privacy and civil liberties.

We believe that the Intelligence Community should develop Privacy and Civil Liberties Impact Assessments for new programs or substantial modifications of existing programs that contain substantial amounts of personally identifiable information. Under the E-Government Act of 2002, federal agencies are required to prepare Privacy Impact Assessments (PIAs) in connection with the procurement of new, or substantially modified, information technology systems. These PIAs are designed to encourage building privacy considerations early into the procurement cycle for such systems.

Our focus here is on the broader programs that may constitute multiple systems. The goal in the program assessment should be broader and more policy-based that has usually been the case for PIAs. For instance, policy officials should explicitly consider the costs and benefits of a program if it unexpectedly becomes public. In some cases, that consideration may result in modifications of the program, or perhaps even in a decision not to go forward with a program.[175]

***Recommendation 36*:** We recommend that for future developments in communications technology, the US should create program-by-program reviews informed by expert technologists, to assess and respond to emerging privacy and civil liberties issues, through the Civil Liberties and Privacy Protection Board or other agencies.

Technical collection and communications technologies continue to evolve rapidly. The US Government should adopt mechanisms that can assess and respond to emerging issues. To do this effectively, expert technologists, with clearances as needed, must be deeply involved in the process.[176]

We recommended in Section VI that the CLPP Board should have an Office of Technology Assessment, capable of assessing the privacy and civil liberties implications of Intelligence Community programs. Sufficient funding for this office should be part of the generally enhanced budget for policy and oversight concerning the expensive and technically sophisticated programs of the Intelligence Community.[177]

SECTION VIII. PROTECTING WHAT WE DO COLLECT

What intelligence and sensitive information the United States does choose to collect or store should be carefully protected from both the Insider Threat and the External Hack. Such protection requires new risk- management approaches to personnel vetting, a change in philosophy about classified networks, and adoption of best commercial practices for highly secure private sector networks.

Our comments in this section deal with personnel with security clearances and classified networks throughout the US Government and not just those in the Intelligence Community. We believe that this broad scope is necessary, and we note that previous reviews have been limited to the Intelligence Community.

In general, we believe that the same standards applied to government employees with security clearances and IT networks with classified information should apply to private sector contractor personnel and networks dealing with Secret and Top Secret data.

A. Personnel Vetting and Security Clearances

***Recommendation 37*:** We recommend that the US Government should move toward a system in which background investigations relating to the vetting of personnel for security clearance are performed solely by US Government employees or by a non-profit, private sector corporation.

***Recommendation 38*:** We recommend that the vetting of personnel for access to classified information should be ongoing, rather than periodic. A standard of Personnel Continuous Monitoring should be adopted, incorporating data from Insider Threat programs and from commercially available sources, to note such things as changes in credit ratings or any arrests or court proceedings.

***Recommendation 39*:** We recommend that security clearances should be more highly differentiated, including the creation of "administrative access" clearances that allow for support and information technology personnel to have the access they need without granting them unnecessary access to substantive policy or intelligence material.

***Recommendation 40*:** We recommend that the US Government should institute a demonstration project in which personnel with security clearances would be given an Access Score, based upon the sensitivity of the information to which they have access and the number and sensitivity of Special Access Programs and Compartmented Material clearances they have. Such an Access Score should be periodically updated.

In the government as in other enterprises, vast stores of information are growing in data bases. Even one unreliable individual with access to parts of a data base may be capable of causing incalculable damage by compromising sensitive information. Unfortunately, almost every agency with sensitive information has experienced a major incident in which a disloyal employee caused significant damage by revealing sensitive data directly or indirectly to another government or to others who would do us harm.

All of the individuals involved in these cases have committed criminal acts after having been vetted by the current security clearance process and, in several well-known cases, after having been polygraphed. Although parts of the Intelligence Community have improved their personnel vetting systems and they may perform well, the general picture throughout the US Government is of an inadequate personnel vetting system.

We believe that the current security clearance personnel vetting practices of most federal departments and agencies are expensive and time- consuming, and that they may not reliably detect the potential for abuse in a timely manner.

The security clearance system should be designed to have an extremely low false-positive rate (granting or continuing a clearance when one should have been denied). Access to sensitive information should be recorded in more detail (e.g. who has access to what and when). The nature and degree of vetting procedures should be adjusted periodically and more closely tied to the sensitivity of the information to which access is granted.

1. How the System Works Now

There are essentially three levels of security clearance (Secret, Top Secret, and Top Secret/SCI). For those obtaining any level of security clearance, the fundamentals of the personnel vetting system are similar.

The applicant is asked to provide the names of a score or more of contacts. An investigator attempts to meet with those people whose names have been provided by the applicant. In many agencies, the investigator is often an employee of a private sector company that is paid by the number of investigations it completes.

If the investigators are unable to meet with the contacts in person, they may in some cases accept a telephone interview. In many agencies, the investigator begins the discussion with all contacts by informing them that anything they say about the applicant can be seen by the applicant because of the requirements of privacy laws. Not surprisingly, very few contacts suggested by the applicant provide derogatory information, especially because they know that their remarks may be disclosed to their friend or acquaintance.

Investigators are required to develop interviewees in addition to those suggested by the applicant. Often the investigator will attempt to inquire of neighbors, those living in the next apartment or house. Increasingly, however, neighbors may not know each other well. Online "friends" sometimes have a better idea about someone than the people living in physical proximity.

As part of an initial security review, investigators may also access some publicly available and commercially available data bases. Such data base reviews are used largely to corroborate information supplied by the applicant on a lengthy questionnaire. Agencies may require a financial disclosure form to be completed, revealing the financial health and holdings of an applicant (although often those declarations are not verified). Some agencies require a polygraph for Top Secret/SCI clearances. Once a clearance has been granted, SECRET- level clearances are often updated only once a decade. Top Secret/SCI clearances may be updated every five years. Random testing for drug use and random polygraphing may occur in between clearance updates.

In many agencies, the current personnel vetting system does not do well in detecting changes in a vetted individual's status after a security clearance has been granted. In most agencies, the security clearance program office might not know if an employee between vettings had just become involved in a bankruptcy, a Driving Under the Influence arrest, a trip to a potentially hostile country, or a conversion to a radical cause such as al-Qa'ida.

Once granted a certain level of clearance because of a need to do part of their jobs, employees are often in a position to read other material at that classification, regardless of its relevance to their job. However, some sensitive projects or sensitive intelligence collection programs ("compartments") have dissemination controls ("bigot lists"). Sometimes access to these programs may be granted based solely on job-related needs and may not trigger an updated or closer review of personnel background material.

As the system works today, the use of special compartmented access programs, limiting access to data, is occasioned often by the means that were employed to collect the information, not by the content of the information, or the target of the collection, or the damage that could be done by unauthorized disclosure of content or target.

2. How the System Might be Improved

A series of broad changes could improve the efficacy of the personnel vetting system.

First, and consistent with practical constraints, agencies and department should move in the direction of reducing or terminating the use of "for-profit" corporations to conduct personnel investigations. When a company is paid upon completion of a case, there is a perverse incentive to complete investigations quickly. For those agencies that cannot do vetting with their own government employee staff, consideration should be given to the creation of a not-for-profit entity modeled on the Federally Funded Research and Development Centers (FFRDC), such as RAND and MITRE, to conduct background investigations and to improve the methodology for doing so. We recommend that a feasibility study be launched in the very near future.

Second, security clearance levels should be further differentiated so that administrative and technical staff who do not require access to the substance of data on a network are given a restricted level of access and security clearance that allows them to do their job, but that does not expose them to sensitive material.

Third, information should be given more restricted handling based not only on how it is collected, but also on the damage that could be created by its compromise.

Fourth, departments and agencies should institute a Work-Related Access approach to the dissemination of sensitive, classified information. While not diminishing the sharing of information between and among agencies, the government should seek to restrict distribution of data to personnel whose jobs actually require access to the information. Typically, analysts working on Africa do not need to read sensitive information about Latin America. Yet in today's system of information-sharing, such "interesting but not essential" data is widely distributed to people who do not really need it.

Implementing this sort of Work-Related Access will necessitate a greater use of Information Rights Management (IRM) software. Greater use of the software means actually widely employing it, not just procuring it. It may also require a significant improvement on the state of the art of such software, as discussed later in this section.

Fifth, we believe that after being granted their initial clearances, all personnel with access to classified information should be included in a Personnel Continuous Monitoring Program (PCMP). The PCMP would access both internally available and commercially available information, such as credit scores, court judgments, traffic violations, and other arrests. The PCMP would include the use of anomaly information from Insider Threat software. When any of these sources of information raised a level of concern, the individual involved would be re-interviewed or subject to further review, within existing employee rights and guidelines.

Sixth, ongoing security clearance vetting of individuals should use a risk-management approach and depend upon the sensitivity and quantity of the programs and information to which they are given access.

We recommend a pilot program of Access Scoring and additional screening for individuals with high scores. Everyone with a security clearance might, for example, be given a regularly updated Access Score, which would vary depending upon the number of special access programs or compartments they are cleared to be in, the sensitivity of the content of those compartments, and the damage that would be done by the compromise of that information.

It would be important that the Access Score be derived not only from the accesses granted by the individual's parent agency, and not only from the list of intelligence programs for which the individual was accredited, but also from all of the restricted programs to which that individual has access from any department, including the Departments of Defense, Energy, Homeland Security, and others.

The greater an individual's Access Score, the more background vetting he or she would be given. Higher scores should require vetting more frequent than the standard interval of five (Top Secret) or 10 (Secret) years. At a certain Access Score level, personnel should be entered into an Additional Monitoring Program. We recognize that such a program could be seen by some as an infringement on the privacy of federal employees and contractors who choose on a voluntary basis to work with highly sensitive information in order to defend our nation. But, employment in government jobs with access to special intelligence or special classified programs is not a right.

Permission to occupy positions of great trust and responsibility is already granted with conditions, including degrees of loss of privacy. In our view, there should be a sliding scale of such conditions depending on the number and sensitivity of the security accesses provided.

We believe that those with the greatest amount of access to sensitive programs and information should be subject to Additional Monitoring, in addition to the PCMP discussed earlier. The routine PCMP review would draw in data on an ongoing basis from commercially available data sources, such as on finances, court proceedings, and driving activity of the sort that is now available to credit scoring and auto insurance companies. Government-provided information might also be added to the data base, such as publicly available information about arrests and data about foreign travel now collected by Customs and Border Patrol.

Those with extremely high Access Scores might be asked to grant permission to the government for their review by a more intrusive Additional Monitoring Program, including random observation of the meta-data related to their personal, home telephone calls, e-mails, use of online social media, and web surfing. Auditing and verification of their Financial Disclosure Forms might also occur.

A data analytics program would be used to sift through the information provided by the Additional Monitoring Program on an ongoing basis to determine if there are correlations that indicate the advisability of some additional review. Usually, any one piece of information obtained by an Additional Monitoring Program would not be determinative of an individual's suitability for special access.

Such a review could involve interviewing the individual involved to obtain an explanation, or contacting her supervisor, or initiating more intrusive vetting. For example, a bankruptcy and a DUI arrest might indicate that the individual is under stress that might necessitate a review of his suitability for sensitive program access. A failure to report a foreign trip as required might trigger a further investigation. Employees whose "outside of work" activities show up in a big data analytics scan as possibly being of concern might have their use of government computers and data bases placed under additional scrutiny. We emphasize that employees with special access must not be stripped of their rights or subjected to Kafkaesque proceedings.

For employees to be willing to participate in a Continuous Monitoring Program, they must know that they will have an opportunity to explain actions that may be flagged by data review.

We have noted that in the wake of recent security violations, some agencies are considering the more extensive use of polygraphy. There are widely varying views about the efficacy of polygraphing, but there can be no disputing that it cannot be a continuous process. It is unable to reveal events which occur after its use. The Personnel Continuous Monitoring Program, with its ongoing ingesting of information from commercial and government data bases, augmented by data analytics, is more likely to reveal any change in the status of an employee between programmed security clearance reviews.

Finally, the security clearance vetting process should also protect the rights of those with access to special programs and information. The President should also ensure that security clearance status not be affected by use of Whistle-Blower, Inspector General, or Congressional Oversight programs (see Appendix D).

About five million people now have active security clearances granted by some arm of the US Government, of which almost 1.5 million have Top Secret clearance. Although we do not have the capability to determine if those numbers are excessive, they certainly seem high. We believe that an interagency committee, representing not just the Intelligence Community, should review in detail why so many personnel require clearances and examine whether there are ways to reduce the total. Such a study may find that many of those with Secret-level clearances could do with a more limited form of access.

Personnel with Security Clearances (10/12)[178]	**Confidential/Secret**	**Top Secret**
Government Employees	2,757,333	791,200
Contractors	582,524	483,263
Other	167,925	135,506
Subtotal	3,507,782	1,409,969
Total	**4,917,751**	

Once granted a clearance, only a very few have had it revoked for cause. Personnel lose clearances mainly because they retire or otherwise leave government service or change jobs. Indeed, many who leave government service manage to maintain their clearances as part-time advisors or by working with contractors. The strikingly small number of people who have their clearances revoked may be because the initial vetting process in all agencies does such a good job and because very few people become security risks after they are initially cleared. But, the numbers suggest to us that the re-vetting process, which usually occurs every five years, may in some agencies not be as rigorous as it should be. Sometimes the initial vetting is assumed to be correct and the only thing that is checked are the "new facts" that have occurred in the preceding five years. Sometimes the reviews that are supposed to take place every five years are delayed. Many agencies do not have a program to obtain some kinds of important information in between security updates.

	Percent of Personnel Whose Security Clearances Were Revoked (FY 12) [179]
CIA	0.4
FBI	0.1
NGA	0.3
NRO	0.5
NSA	0.3
State	0.1

3. Information Sharing

Recommendation 41: We recommend that the "need-to-share" or "need-to-know" models should be replaced with a Work-Related Access model, which would ensure that all personnel whose role requires access to specific information have such access, without making the data more generally available to cleared personnel who are merely interested.

Classified information should be shared only with those who genuinely need to know. Beyond the use of compartments, however, the vast bulk of classified information is broadly available to people with security clearances. Analyses of the failure to prevent the September 11th, 2001 attacks concluded that information about those individuals involved in the plot had not been shared appropriately between and among agencies. Although some of that lack of sharing reflected intentional, high- level decisions, other data was not made broadly available because of a system that made it difficult to disseminate some kinds of information across agencies. Thus, after the attacks, the mantra "Need to Share" replaced the previous concept of "Need to Know."

In some contexts, that new approach may have gone too far or been too widely misunderstood. The "Need to Share" called for the distribution of relevant information to personnel with a job/task defined requirement for such information. It did not call for the profligate distribution of classified information to anyone with a security clearance and an interest in reading the information.

The problem with the "need-to-share" principle is that it gives rise to a multitude of other risks. Consistent with the goal of risk management, the appropriate guideline is that *information should be shared only with those who need to know*. There is no good reason to proliferate the number of people with whom information is shared if some or many of those people do not need or use that information in their work. The principle of "need to share" can endanger privacy, heighten the risk of abuse, endanger public trust, and increase insider threats.

To be sure, the matching of one agency's records against another agency's records—for example, comparing fingerprints collected off of bomb fragments in Afghanistan to fingerprints culled at US border crossings—is one of the most important information tools we have in combating terrorism. Such sharing must continue, but can (and often does) take place on a machine-to-machine basis with strict control on which human beings can obtain access to the data.

To its credit, the Intelligence Community has been taking steps to restrict the number of people who have access to confidential or classified information. We applaud these steps. We recommend that seemingly compelling arguments about the importance of information-sharing should be qualified by a recognition that information should not be shared with those who do not have a genuine need to know.

B. Network Security[180]

***Recommendation 42*:** We recommend that the Government networks carrying Secret and higher classification information should use the best available cyber security hardware, software, and procedural protections against both external and internal threats. The National Security Advisor and the Director of the Office of Management and Budget should annually report to the President on the implementation of this standard.

All networks carrying classified data, including those in contractor corporations, should be subject to a Network Continuous Monitoring Program, similar to the EINSTEIN 3 and TUTELAGE programs, to record network traffic for real time and subsequent review to detect anomalous activity, malicious actions, and data breaches.

***Recommendation 43*:** We recommend that the President's prior directions to improve the security of classified networks, Executive Order 13587, should be fully implemented as soon as possible.

***Recommendation 44*:** We recommend that the National Security Council Principals Committee should annually meet to review the state of security of US Government networks carrying classified information, programs to improve such security, and evolving threats to such networks. An interagency "Red Team" should report annually to the Principals with an independent, "second opinion" on the state of security of the classified information networks.

***Recommendation 45*:** We recommend that all US agencies and departments with classified information should expand their use of software, hardware, and procedures that limit access to documents and data to those specifically authorized to have access to them. The US Government should fund the development of, procure, and widely use on classified networks improved Information Rights Management software to control the dissemination of classified data in a way that provides greater restrictions on access and use, as well as an audit trail of such use.

Information technology (IT) has become so central to the functioning of the government in general and national security in particular that policy officials need to be conversant with the technology. No longer can senior officials relegate concerns about IT networks to management or administrative staff. Policy officials are ultimately responsible for the IT networks of their organizations. They need to understand the systems and issues raised by technologists.

Toward that end, technologists should be part of more policy, decision-making, and oversight processes. Similarly, national security policy officials need to take the time to understand in detail how the various components of the Intelligence Community work, and especially how their collection programs operate.

The security of classified networks is, in the age of cyber war, one of the highest priorities in national security. Nonetheless, the status of security improvement and the state of the cyber defenses of our sensitive networks have not been a topic for regular review by senior interagency policy officials. Department and agency leaders have also had little way to verify if the reports of their subordinates concerning the security of their classified networks are entirely accurate or complete.

We recommend that there be an annual review by NSC Principals of the security of classified networks and the implementation of programmed upgrades. To inform the principals' discussion, we also recommend that the staffs of OMB and NSC lead a process to identify issues and potential deficiencies. We also suggest that a "Red Team" be created to provide a second opinion to Principals on the security vulnerabilities of all classified networks.

The security of government networks carrying classified information has traditionally been outward looking. It was assumed that anyone who had access to the network had been subjected to extensive vetting and was therefore trustworthy and reliable.

There are two flaws in that thinking. First, as has been demonstrated, some people who have been given Top Secret/SCI clearances are not trustworthy. Second, it may be possible for unauthorized individuals to gain access to the classified networks and to assume the identity of an authorized user. The government's classified networks require immediate internal hardening.

Beyond measures designed to control access to data on networks, there is a need to increase the security of the classified networks in general. Many of the US Government's networks would benefit from a major technological refresh, to use newer and less vulnerable versions of operating systems, to adopt newer security software proven in the private sector, and to re-architect network designs to employ such improvements as Thin Client and air-gapped approaches.

Despite what some believe is the inherent security of classified networks, as the so-called Buckshot Yankee incident demonstrated, it is possible for foreign powers to penetrate US networks carrying classified information. Just as some foreign powers regularly attempt to penetrate private sector networks in the US to steal intellectual property and research, others are engaged in frequent attempts to penetrate US networks with secret data.

To improve the security of classified networks, we believe that such networks should be given at least as much internal and external security as the most secure, unclassified networks in the private sector. Although many US corporations have inadequate network security, some in financial services have achieved a high level of assurance through the use of a risk management approach. State-of-the-art cyber security products used in private sector companies are not as often used on classified US Government networks as we would have believed likely.

We believe that inadequacy can be explained by two factors: 1) classified network administrators have traditionally focused on perimeter network defenses and 2) the procurement process in the government is too lengthy and too focused on large-scale system integrator contracts that do not easily allow for the agile adoption of new security products that keep up with the ever-changing threat. In our view, every department and agency's IT security budget and procurement processes ought to include funding set aside and procedures for the rapid acquisition and installation of newly developed security products related to recently appearing threats. These systems should be reviewed and procurement measures made through a decision making process that considers cost-benefit analysis, cost-effectiveness, and risk management.

1. Executive Order 13578

In recognition of the need to improve security on government networks with classified data, President Obama issued Executive Order 13587 to improve the security of classified networks against the Insider Threat. We have found that the implementation of that directive has been at best uneven and far too slow. Every day that it remains unimplemented, sensitive data, and therefore potentially lives, are at risk. Interagency implementation monitoring was not performed at a sufficiently high level in OMB or the NSS. The Administration did not direct the re-programming of adequate funds. Officials who were tardy in compliance were not held accountable. No central staff was created to enforce implementation or share best practices and lessons learned.

The implementation of Executive Order 13587 is in marked contrast to the enforcement of compliance with a somewhat similar effort, the conversion of government networks for Y2K. The Y2K software upgrades were carried out under the aegis of Executive Order 13073, issued only 22 months before the implementation deadline. That order established an Interagency Council co-chaired by an Assistant to the President and by the Director of OMB. It required quarterly reports to the President.

We believe that the implementation of Executive Order 13578 should be greatly accelerated, that deadlines should be moved up and enforced, and the adequate funding should be made available within agency budget ceilings and a Deputy Assistant to the President might be directed to enforce implementation. The interagency process might be co-led by the Deputy Director of OMB.

In addition to the Insider Threat measures discussed above, we believe that government classified networks could have their overall security improved by, among other steps, priority implementation of the following:

- Network Continuous Monitoring techniques on all classified networks similar to the EINSTEIN-TUTELAGE Program now being implemented on US Government unclassified networks and the systems of certain private sector, critical infrastructure companies.
- A Security Operations Center (SOC) with real-time visibility on all classified US Government networks. There are now many SOCs, but no one place where fusion and total visibility takes place; and
- More severe limits on the movement of data from unclassified to classified networks. Although such data being uploaded is scanned today, the inspection is unlikely to detect a Zero Day threat (i.e. malicious software that has not been seen before).

2. Physical and Logical Separation

We believe that the most cost-effective efforts to enhance the security of IT networks carrying classified data are likely to be those that create greater physical and logical separation of data, through network segmentation, encryption, identity access management, access control to data, limitation of data storage on clients, and "air-gapping." Among the measures we suggest be more carefully considered are:

- The creation of Project Enclaves on networks, with firewalls, access control lists, and multi-factor (including biometric) authentication required for entry.
- Project-based encryption for data at rest and in use. Today, most data at rest on classified networks is not encrypted (although the networks and the data in transit are). Encrypting data whether at rest or in transit and linking that encryption with Identity Access Management (IAM) or IRM software would prevent reading by those not authorized even if they do access the data.
- IRM. To determine and limit who has access to data in a Project Based Encryption file, agencies should be encouraged to consider the use of IRM software that specifies what groups or individuals may read, or forward, or edit, or copy, or print, or download a document.

  IRM is known by other terms, such as Digital Rights Management, in some agencies. The IRM software should be linked to a multi-factor Identity Access Management system so that administrative and technical staff, such as System Administrators, and others cannot access the content of the data.
- Separation of Networks. Networks can be physically separated to varying degrees, from using separate colors on a fiber to using different fibers, to using different physical paths. In true "air- gapping," a network shares no physical devices whatsoever with other networks. In logical separation, networks may be maintained separate by firewalls, access controls, identity access management systems, and encryption.

  We believe that every relevant agency should conduct a review using cost-benefit analysis, and risk- management principles to determine if it would make sense to achieve greater security by further physical and logical separation of networks carrying data of highly sensitive programs.

We have found that there are few choices and perhaps insufficiently robust products today among Identity Rights Management software and among Insider Threat Anomaly Detection software.

We believe that the government should fast track the development of Next-Generation IRM and Next-Generation Insider Threat software, waiving the normal research and procurement rules and timetables. The development of NextGen software in these areas should not, however, be an excuse for failure to deploy the software that is now available.

Fortunately, the government itself may have developed the basis for a more robust IRM software. The National Institute for Standards and Technology (NIST) of the Department of Commerce has created an Open Source platform for Next-Generation IRM software. Private sector developers should be granted access to that platform quickly, as well as encouraged to develop their own systems.

The NIST open source software, like other software now being used in some agencies, prevents the downloading of sensitive data from central servers. Analysts may access the data and employ it, but may not transfer it. With the NIST software, the user sees an image of the data, but is unable to download it to a client and then to a thumb drive, CD, or other media. In general, we believe that sensitive data should reside only on servers and not on clients.

IRM systems and "data-on-server only" policies allow for auditing of data access, but they also generally presume the use of a data-tagging system when data is initially ingested into a network or system.

We believe that additional work needs to be done to make that phase of data control less onerous, complex, and time-consuming. Government-sponsored development or procurement would promote the more rapid solution of those problems with data tagging.

NSA, among others, is returning to the Thin Client architecture, which many agencies abandoned 15-20 years ago in favor of cheaper, Commercial Off The Shelf (COTS) models. In the Thin Client architecture, the user may employ any screen on the network after properly authenticating.

The screens, however, are "dumb terminals" with little software loaded on the devices. All applications and data are stored on servers, which are easier to secure and monitor than are large numbers of distributed clients. The use of a Thin Client architecture is, we believe, a more secure approach for classified networks and should be more widely used.

C. Cost-Benefit Analysis and Risk Management

***Recommendation 46*:** We recommend the use of cost-benefit analysis and risk-management approaches, both prospective and retrospective, to orient judgments about personnel security and network security measures.

In our statement of principles, we have emphasized that in many domains, public officials rely on a careful analysis of both costs and benefits. In our view, both prospective and retrospective analysis have important roles to play in the domain under discussion, though they also present distinctive challenges, above all because of limits in available knowledge and challenges in quantifying certain variables. In particular, personnel security and network security measures should be subject to careful analysis of both benefits and costs (to the extent feasible).

Monetary costs certainly matter; public and private resources are limited. When new security procedures are put in place—for example, to reduce insider threats—the cost may well be ascertainable. It may be possible to identify a range, with upper and lower bounds. But the benefits of security procedures are likely to be more challenging to specify. It remains difficult, even today, to quantify the damage done by the recent leaks of NSA material. In principle, the question is the magnitude of the harm that is averted by new security procedures.

Because those procedures may discourage insider threats from materializing, it will not be feasible to identify some averted harms.

Even if so, some analysis should be possible. For example, officials should be able to see to what extent new security procedures are helpful in detecting behavior with warning signs. Retrospective analysis can improve judgments by showing what is working and what is not. Risk-management approaches generally suggest hedging strategies on investment in preventative measures when detailed actuarial data are not available. That approach, along with breakeven analysis,[181] may be necessary when considering risk contingencies that have never come to fruition in the past.

CONCLUSION

In this Report, we have explored both continuity and change. The continuity involves enduring values, which we have traced to the founding of the American republic. When the Constitution was ratified, We the People—in whom sovereignty resides—made commitments, at once, to the protection of the common defense, securing the blessings of liberty, and ensuring that people are "secure in their persons, houses, papers, and effects." In the American tradition, liberty and security need not be in conflict. They can be mutually supportive.

This understanding lies at the foundation of our culture and our rights, and it is shared by many of our close friends and allies.

At the same time, we live in a period of astonishingly rapid change. We face new threats to the common defense, including those that come from terrorism. For those who seek to do us harm, new technologies provide unprecedented opportunities for coordination across space and time, and also for identifying potential vulnerabilities. For the United States, our allies, and others whom we seek to protect, those very technologies provide opportunities to identify threats and to eliminate them. And in light of the pace of change, there is no question that today's technologies, extraordinary though they are, will seem hopelessly primitive in the relatively near future—and that both the threats and the opportunities will expand accordingly.

We have emphasized the importance of careful assessment of the real-world consequences of our choices, and of a willingness to reassess those choices as new information is obtained.

Our goal in this Report has been to promote enduring values in a period of rapid change, and to assert that those values are essentially timeless. We have identified a series of reforms that are designed to safeguard the privacy and dignity of American citizens, and to promote public trust, while also allowing the Intelligence Community to do what must be done to respond to genuine threats.

No nation treats citizens of other nations the same way that it treats its own people, but we have emphasized that numerous steps can and should be taken to protect the privacy and dignity of citizens of other nations, including those who are outside the United States. We have also emphasized that surveillance should never be undertaken to promote illegitimate goals, such as the theft of trade secrets or the suppression of freedom of speech or religion.

We have also called for institutional reforms designed to ensure that NSA remains a foreign intelligence collection agency and that other institutions, both independent and inside the Executive Branch, work to protect privacy and civil liberty. We have stressed that it is exceedingly important to maintain a secure and open Internet, and several of our recommendations are designed to promote that goal. Protection of what we collect is indispensable to safeguarding national security, privacy, and public trust; the recommendations made here would significantly strengthen existing protections.

We have emphasized throughout that the central task is one of managing a wide assortment of risks. We are hopeful that the recommendations made here might prove helpful in striking the right balance. Free nations must protect themselves, and nations that protect themselves must remain free.

APPENDIX A. THE LEGAL STANDARDS FOR GOVERNMENT ACCESS TO COMMUNICATIONS

There is considerable complexity in the legal standards for government access to communications-related information. This Appendix seeks to make the legal requirements and possible reforms easier to understand. This is achieved by setting forth an outline consisting of four components.

This short appendix can only set forth certain key elements of the law and is not aimed at representing a comprehensive picture of all relevant statutory provisions and jurisprudence.

The first component sets forth the burden of proof that the government must meet in order to obtain the information. From less strict to stricter, the burden of proof used in this area of law includes: (1) relevant; (2) reasonable grounds to believe, or reasonable and articulable suspicion; and (3) probable cause.

The second component sets forth the scope of the activity to which the burden of proof applies, such as a criminal investigation or foreign intelligence investigation. Both a law enforcement and FISA warrant require "probable cause." The probable cause is of a different thing, however.

For a criminal warrant there must be probable cause that a crime has been, is, or will be committed. For a FISA warrant, there must be probable cause that the target is an agent of a foreign power.

The third component sets forth the level of authorization required to undertake the activity. The decision is sometimes made by the analyst, or subject to approval within the executive branch, or subject to approval by a judge.

The fourth component is the nature of the information that can be obtained pursuant to the relevant legal authority.

If policymakers wish to raise the standards for government access, one or more of the first three components can be amended. For instance, a standard could be raised to probable cause, the scope of investigation could be narrowed, or higher-level approval could be required.

Similarly, easing the standards could occur along one or more of these three dimensions.

For instance, relevance might be required rather than a stricter standard, or the scope of the investigation could broaden, or no sign-off by higher authority would be needed.

This appendix sets forth the standards for law enforcement's undertaking of criminal investigations and the intelligence community's foreign intelligence investigations. The standards presented below are in some instances simplified, so the applicable statutes and case law should be consulted for further details.

Law Enforcement Purposes

Traditional Warrant: (1) Probable cause. (2) Crime has been, is, or will be committed. (3) Order from a judge or, in the language of the Fourth Amendment, a "neutral magistrate." (4) Can obtain documents, records, or things.

Wiretap (18 U.S.C. § 2518): (1) Probable cause, plus additional requirements such as other investigatory methods are unlikely to succeed. (2) Crime has been, is, or will be committed, only for crimes listed in 18 U.S.C. § 2516. (3) Order issued by judge. (4) Conversations that are evidence of criminal activity.

Pen/Trap (18 U.S.C. § 3122): (1) Relevant. (2) Ongoing criminal investigation. (3) Order issued by Judge. (4) Communications meta-data (dialing, routing, addressing, and signaling information but not content).

Required Disclosure of Customer Communications Records (18 U.S.C. § 2703(d)): (1) Specific and articulable facts that there are reasonable grounds to believe relevant and material. (2) Ongoing criminal investigation. (3) Order issued by Judge. (4) Various classes of records, including opened e- mails if there is notice to the subscriber and non-content records with no notice requirement.

Intelligence Purposes

Title I FISA (50 U.S.C. § 1801): (1) Probable cause. (2) Target is an agent of a foreign power or a foreign power and each of the facilities or places is used or about to be used by a foreign power or an agent of a foreign power. (3) Order issued by FISC pursuant to AG certification. (4) Contents of communications.

Pen/Trap FISA (50 U.S.C. § 1842): (1) Relevant to an ongoing investigation. (2) To protect against international terrorism or clandestine intelligence activities, or to obtain foreign intelligence information not concerning a US person. (3) Order issued by FISC pursuant to AG certification. (4) Communications meta-data (but not content).

FISA Section 702 (50 U.S.C. § 1881): (1) Reasonable belief person is non-US Person located outside the US and subject to one of the FISC-approved certifications. (2) To acquire foreign intelligence. (3) Targeting requested by analyst subject to review by adjudicators. (4) Content of communications.

Section 215 (50 U.S.C. § 1861): (1) Reasonable grounds to believe that the tangible things sought are relevant. (2) To obtain foreign intelligence information about a non-US person or to protect against international terrorism or clandestine intelligence activities relevant to an authorized investigation. (3) Order issued by FISC pursuant to AG certification. (4) Documents, records, or other tangible things.

National Security Letters (50 U.S.C. § 436): (1) Relevant or pursuant to an open national security investigation. (2) For counterintelligence and counterterrorism, including cyber investigations. (3) FBI Special Agent in Charge or more senior FBI official. (4) Communications meta-data. Note: Other NSL statutes exists for other categories of records.

Executive Order 12333: (1) No requirement. (2) For foreign intelligence or counterintelligence purposes. (3) Decided by analyst with supervisory approval pursuant to internal guidelines. (4) Foreign intelligence information.

APPENDIX B.

Overview of NSA Privacy Protections under FAA 702

TARGETING	• Targeting must be for a valid foreign intelligence purpose in response to National Intelligence Priorities. • Targeting must be under a Foreign Intelligence Surveillance Court (FISC)-approved FAA 702 Certification and limited to non–US Persons located overseas. • All targeting is governed by FISC-approved targeting procedures.	• Targeting of US Persons or any persons located inside the United States is strictly prohibited. • Reverse-targeting of US Persons is prohibited.
COLLECTION	• Specific communications identifiers (for example, phone numbers or e-mail addresses) are used to limit collection only to communications to, from, or about a valid foreign intelligence target.	• Intentional collection of wholly domestic communications (that is, all communicants are in the US) is prohibited.
ANALYSIS/ EXPLORATION	• Queries into collected data must be designed to return valid foreign intelligence. • Overly broad queries are prohibited.	• Upon additional authorization and oversight, queries using US Person identifiers are permitted for foreign intelligence purposes. • Any wholly domestic communications (that is, all communicants are in the United States) must be destroyed upon recognition.
DISSEMINATION	• Disseminations to external entities, including Executive Branch agencies and select foreign partners, are made for valid foreign intelligence purposes.	• US Person information is protected in reporting unless necessary to understand and assess the foreign intelligence, evidence of a crime, or other exception applies.
RETENTION	• Raw data is destroyed after two years or five years (depending on the collection source) after the expiration of the certification under which it was acquired.	

Disclaimer: This overview is a quick reference guide and is not intended as a substitute for the minimization procedures and their implementation.

Overview of NSA Privacy Protections under EO 12333

TARGETING	• Targeting must be for a valid foreign intelligence purpose in response to National Intelligence Priorities. • All targeting is governed by DOD regulations and Attorney General–approved procedures.	• Targeting of US Persons is NOT permitted except in limited circumstances that require additional authorization or consent.
COLLECTION	• Selection terms/identifiers must be crafted to limit collection—to the extent possible—to communications responsive to a valid foreign intelligence purpose.	
ANALYSIS/ EXPLORSATION	• Queries into collected data must be designed to return valid foreign intelligence. • Overly broad queries are prohibited.	• Queries for US Person information are prohibited except in limited circumstances that require additional authorization or consent. • Any wholly domestic communication (that is, all communicants are in the United States) must be destroyed upon recognition.
DISSEMINATION	• Disseminations to external entities, including Executive Branch agencies and select foreign partners, are made for valid foreign intelligence purposes.	• US Person information is protected in reporting unless necessary to understand and assess the foreign intelligence, evidence of a crime, or other exception applies.
RETENTION	• Raw data is destroyed after five years except when necessary to maintain technical databases for cryptanalytic or traffic analysis purposes.	

Disclaimer: This overview is a quick reference guide and is not intended as a substitute for the minimization procedures and their implementation.

APPENDIX C. US INTELLIGENCE: MULTIPLE LAYERS OF RULES AND OVERSIGHT

The graphic below illustrates the role played by each of the three branches of the US Government in governance of a query run by an intelligence analyst. On the left are the laws and guidelines that apply to actions of the analyst, setting forth the parameters within which the search may be conducted. The right side of the graphic highlights the review, oversight, and auditing functions of each of the three branches, once the search has been conducted.

Guidance to the IC

LEGISLATIVE BRANCH

- Constitution
- Statutes

JUDICIAL BRANCH

- Court orders and standard minimization procedures

EXECUTIVE BRANCH

- Executive Orders and Presidential Directives
- Attorney General Guidelines
- IC Directives
- Agency regulations, instructions, and policies
- Agency training and guidance

Analyst

Oversight and Enforcemen

LEGISLATIVE BRANCH

- Congress[a]

JUDICIAL BRANCH

- Foreign Intelligence[b]

EXECUTIVE BRANCH

- Privacy and Civil Liberties Oversight Board[c]
- President's Intelligence Oversight Board[d]
- Department of Justice[e]
- ODNI-level officials[f]
- Department-level officials[g]
- Agency-level officials[h]

[a] Determines whether and how to authorize/fund intelligence activities and conducts oversight via intelligence and other committees.

[b] Rules on matters under Foreign Intelligence Surveillance Act.

[c] Provides privacy/civil liberties advice and oversight for USG efforts to protect the nation from terrorism.

[d] Reviews reports of potential violations of law and executive order on behalf of President.

[e] Includes DOJ's National Security Division and DOJ's Privacy and Civil Liberties Office.

[f] Includes ODNI's Civil Liberties and Privacy Office, ODNI/OGC, and the IC Inspector General.

[g] At the department level, these can include departmental counterparts to the agency-level organizations, and may also include other offices (for example, DOD's Assistant to the Secretary of Defense for Intelligence oversight).

[h] At the agency level, these can include the following organizations: Offices of General Counsel, Offices of Inspector General, Civil Liberties and Privacy Offices, Intelligence Oversight Offices, Compliance Offices (for example, NSA's new Civil Liberties and Privacy Officer position, and NSA's Office of the Director of Compliance).

APPENDIX D. AVENUES FOR WHISTLE-BLOWERS IN THE INTELLIGENCE COMMUNITY

Employee Protections For Disclosures:

- National Security Act of 1947, CIA Act of 1949, Inspector General Act of 1978
- Presidential Policy Directive No. 19
- Agencies' Internal Policies

APPENDIX E. US GOVERNMENT ROLE IN CURRENT ENCRYPTION STANDARDS

NSA provided the Review Group the following information, outlining the reliability of certain encryption systems. Our recommendation 31 would give the force of law to prohibitions on undercutting these and other standards.

Most of the standards described below are approved by NIST for protecting unclassified US Government information and by NSA for protecting classified US Government information. AES, SHA-2, EC-DSA, and EC-DH make up the core of "Suite B," NSA's mandated set of public standard algorithms, approved in 2006, for protecting classified information.[182] Each algorithm discussed below is currently in use in National Security Systems, although NSA is pursuing the transition from SHA-1 to SHA-2. For further information on all but SHA-1 see https://www.cnss.gov/policies.html and references contained there.

In general, NSA applies the deep cryptanalytic tradecraft and mathematical expertise developed over decades of making and breaking codes, to ensure that cryptography standardized by the US Government is strong enough to protect its own sensitive communications.

AES – The Advanced Encryption Standard – FIPS 197

NSA did not contribute to nor modify the design of the Advanced Encryption Standard (AES). It was designed by two European cryptographers: Joan Daemen and Vincent Rijmen.

It was published and submitted in 1998 for NIST's AES competition and selected in 2001 as the Advanced Encryption Standard. NSA extensively examined the algorithms in the competition and provided technical guidance to NIST during the competition to make sure that NIST's final selection was a secure algorithm. NIST made the final algorithm choice under its own authority, independent of NSA. Both NSA and the academic cryptography community have thoroughly analyzed the AES.

RSA – The Rivest, Shamir, Adelman Public Key Algorithm – FIPS 186, NIST SP 800-56B

NSA did not contribute to, nor modify, the design of RSA, but it did provide input on RSA usage in standards. It was designed in 1977 by three cryptographers working at MIT: Americans Ron Rivest, and Leonard Adelman, and Israeli Adi Shamir. The algorithm was independently designed earlier by Cliff Cocks of UK GCHQ in 1973 but was not published, and was only declassified in 1997. Both NSA and the academic cryptography community have thoroughly analyzed the RSA algorithm both as a digital signature (FIPS-186) and as an encryption algorithm for keys (SP 800-56B).

Diffie-Hellman/Elliptic Curve Diffie-Hellman – The Diffie-Hellman Key Exchange Algorithm – NIST SP 800-56A

NSA did not contribute to, nor modify, the design of Diffie-Hellman. The Diffie-Hellman Key Exchange Algorithm was designed by American cryptographer Whitfield Diffie and Martin Hellman at Stanford University in 1976. It was invented by Malcolm Williamson of GCHQ a few years earlier, but never published. The elliptic curve variant of the Diffie-Hellman key exchange was invented independently by American cryptographers Victor Miller and Neal Koblitz in 1985. NSA ensured that a class of potentially weak elliptic curve parameters was not included in the NIST standard. Both NSA and the academic cryptography community have thoroughly analyzed both the Diffie-Hellman Key Exchange algorithm and its elliptic curve variant (both found in NIST SP 800-56A).

DSA/ECDSA—The Digital Signature Algorithm/Elliptic Curve DSA — FIPS 186

NSA designed the algorithm known as DSA as the original signature algorithm in FIPS 186 initially in 1991-1993, then contributed advice on later versions of the standard. NSA also designed a variant of DSA that uses the mathematics of elliptic curves and is known as the "Elliptic Curve DSA" or ECDSA. Both NSA and the academic cryptography community have thoroughly analyzed the DSA (FIPS 186).

SHA-1 – The Secure Hash Algorithm Variant 1 – FIPS 180-1

NSA designed the SHA-1 algorithm as a correction to the SHA-0 algorithm, a longer (160-bit) variant of the MD5 algorithm designed by Ron Rivest. SHA-0 was an NSA design standardized in 1993. In 1994, NSA acted quickly to replace SHA-0 with SHA-1 as a NIST standard when NSA cryptanalysts discovered a problem with the SHA-0 design that reduced its security. Both NSA and the academic cryptography community have thoroughly analyzed the SHA-1 (FIPS 180). For many years NIST and NSA have recommended that people stop using SHA-1 and start using the SHA- 2 hash algorithms.

SHA-2 – The Secure Hash Algorithm Variant 2 – FIPS 180-2

NSA designed the four different-length hash algorithms contained in FIPS- 180-2 and collectively known as SHA-2. Because of their longer hash lengths (224, 256, 384, and 512 bits), the SHA-2 hash lengths provide greater security than SHA-1. SHA-2 also blocks some algorithm weaknesses in the SHA-1 design. These algorithms were standardized in 2002. Both NSA and the academic cryptography community have thoroughly analyzed the SHA-2 hash algorithms (FIPS 180).

APPENDIX F. REVIEW GROUP BRIEFINGS AND MEETINGS

Government

Executive Branch

Assistant to the President for Homeland Security & Counterterrorism
Bureau of Alcohol, Tobacco, Firearms and Explosives
Central Intelligence Agency
Defense Intelligence Agency
Department of Commerce
Department of Defense
Department of Homeland Security
Department of Justice
Department of State
Drug Enforcement Agency
Federal Bureau of Investigations
National Archives and Records Administration
National Counterterrorism Center
National Institute for Standards and Technology
National Reconnaissance Office
National Security Advisor
National Security Agency
Office of the Director of National Intelligence
President's Intelligence Advisory Board

Privacy and Civil Liberties Oversight Board
Program Manager for the Information Sharing Environment (PM-ISE)
Special Assistant to the President for Cyber Security
Treasury Department

Legislative Branch

House Judiciary Committee
House Permanent Select Committee on Intelligence
Senate Judiciary Committee
Senate Select Committee on Intelligence

Judicial Branch

Judge John D. Bates, United States District Court Judge (former Foreign Intelligence Surveillance Court Judge)

Private Entities

Organizations

American Civil Liberties Union
Apple
AT&T
Brennan Center for Justice
CATO Institute
Center for Democracy & Technology
Center for National Security Studies
Electronic Frontier Foundation
Electronic Privacy Information Center
Enterprise Risk Management/Root Cause Analysis
Facebook
Google
Human Rights Watch
IBM Center for Excellence
Information Technology and Innovation Foundation
Information Technology Industry Council
Microsoft
New America Foundation
Open Technology Institute
Palantir
Rackspace
Reporters Committee for Freedom of the Press
Software & Information Industry Association
the TOR Project
Verizon
Yahoo

Individuals

Baker, Stewart; Steptoe & Johnson
Berman, Jerry
Blaze, Matt; University of Pennsylvania
Bowden, Caspar
Cate, Fred; Indiana University
Donohue, Laura; Georgetown Law School
Farber, David; Carnegie Mellon University
Felten, Ed; Princeton University
Klein, Hans; Georgia Institute of Technology
Kris, David; Intellectual Ventures (Former DoJ NSD Chief)
Malinowski, Tom; Human Rights Watch former director
Soltani, Ashkan
Wittes, Ben; Brookings Institution
Wolf, Christopher; Hogan, Lovells

Foreign Organizations

(LIBE) European Parliament Committee on Civil Liberties, Justice, and Home Affairs
European Union Privacy & Civil Liberties delegation

APPENDIX G. GLOSSARY

A *(AES) Advanced Encryption Standard* An encryption algorithm for securing sensitive but unclassified material by US Government agencies and, as a consequence, may eventually become the de facto encryption standard for commercial transactions in the private sector.
Source: http://searchsecurity.techtarget.com/definition.Advanced-Encryption-Standard
AG Attorney General

B *Backdoor* A means of access to a computer program that bypasses security mechanisms. A programmer may sometimes install a back door so that the program can be accessed for troubleshooting or other purposes.
Source: http://searchsecurity.techtarget.com/definition/back-door
Big Data Analytics The process of examining large amounts of data of a variety of types (big data) to uncover hidden patterns, unknown correlations, and other useful information.
Source: http://searchbusinessanalytics.techtarget.com/definition/big-data- analytics
Bulk Data An electronic collection of data composed of information from multiple records, whose primary relationship to each other is their shared origin from a single or multiple databases.
Source: http://www.maine.gov/legis/opla/RTKINFORMEcomments.pdf

C *Church Committee* An 11-member investigating body of the Senate (a Senate Select Committee) that studied governmental operations with respect to Intelligence Activities. Itpublished 14 reports that contain a wealth of information on the formation, operation, and abuses of US intelligence agencies. The reports were published in 1975 and 1976, after which recommendations for reform were debated in Congress and in some cases enacted.
Source: http://www.aarclibrary.org/publib/contents/church/contents_church_reports.htm
CIA Central Intelligence Agency
Cloud Computing A model for enabling ubiquitous, convenient, on- demand network access to a shared pool of configurable computing resources (e.g., networks, servers, storage, applications, and services) that can be rapidly provisioned and released with minimal management effort or service provider interaction.
Source: http://csrc.nist.gov/publications/nistpubs/800-145/SP800-145.pdf
CLPP Board Civil Liberties and Privacy Protection Board
(CMP) Continuous Monitoring Program Maintaining ongoing awareness of information security, vulnerabilities, and threats to support organizational risk management decisions.
Source: http://csrc.nist.gov/publications/nistpubs/800-137/SP800-137- Final.pdf
Counter-intelligence Information gathered and activities conducted to identify, deceive, exploit, disrupt, or protect against espionage, other intelligence activities, sabotage, or assassinations conducted for or on behalf of foreign powers, organizations or persons, or their agents, or international terrorist organizations or activities.
Source: (Executive Order 12333, as amended 30 July 2008 and JP 2-01.2, CI & HUMINT in Joint Operations, 11 Mar 2011)
http://www.fas.org/irp/eprint/ci-glossary.pdf
Counter-proliferation Those actions (e.g., detect and monitor, prepare to conduct counter-proliferation operations, offensive operations, weapons of mass destruction, active defense, and passive defense) taken to defeat the threat and/or use of weapons of mass destruction against the United States, our military forces, friends, and allies.
Source: (JP 1-02 & JP 3-40)
http://www.fas.org/irp/eprint/ci-glossary.pdf

D Data Mining The process of collecting, searching through, and analyzing a large amount of data within a database, to discover patterns of relationships.
Source: http://dictionary.reference.com/browse/data+mining?s=t
Decryption The process of converting encrypted data back to its original form, so it can be understood.
Source: http://searchsecurity.techtarget.com/definition/encryption
DHS Department of Homeland Security
DIAA Defense Information Assurance Agency
Diffie-Hellman Key Exchange Algorithm Cryptographic algorithm used for secure key exchange. The algorithm allows two users to exchange a symmetric secret key through an insecure wired or wireless channel and without any prior secrets.

Source: (2005 International Conference on Wireless Networks, Communications and Mobile Computing)
http://ieeexplore.ieee.org/xpls/abs_all.jsp?arnumber=1549408 &tag=1
(DRM) Digital Rights Management/ (IRM) Information Rights Management A collection of systems and software applications used to protect the copyrights of documents and electronic media. These include digital music and movies, as well as other data that is stored and transferred digitally. DRM is important to publisher of electronic media because it helps to control the trading, protection, monitoring, and tracking of digital media, limiting the illegal propagation of copyrighted works. Source: http://www.techterms.com/definitions/drm
DISA Defense Information Systems Agency
DNI Director of National Intelligence
DOD Department of Defense
DOJ Department of Justice
DTRA Defense Threat Reduction Agency

E *Einstein 3* An advanced, network-layer intrusion detection system (IDS) which analyzes Internet traffic as it moves in and out of United States Federal Government networks. EINSTEIN filters packets at the gateway and reports anomalies to the United States Computer Emergency Readiness Team (US-CERT) at the Department of Homeland Security.
Source: http://searchsecurity.techtarget.com/definition/Einstein
Encryption The conversion of data into a form, called a ciphertext (encrypted text), that cannot be easily understood by unauthorized people.
Source: http://searchsecurity.techtarget.com/definition/encryption
Executive Order Official documents, numbered consecutively, through which the President of the United States manages the operations of the Federal Government.
Source: http://www.archives.gov/federal-register/executive- orders/about.html
Executive Order 12333 Under section 2.3, intelligence agencies can only collect, retain, and disseminate information about a "US person" (US citizens and lawful permanent residents) if permitted by applicable law, if the information fits within one of the enumerated categories under Executive Order 12333, and if it is permitted under that agency's implementing guidelines approved by the Attorney General. The EO has been amended to reflect the changing security and intelligence environment and structure within the US Government.
Source: https://it.ojp.gov/default.aspx?area=privacy&page=1261#12333

F *FBI* Federal Bureau of Investigation
(FISA) Foreign Intelligence Surveillance Act As amended, establishes procedures for the authorization of electronic surveillance, use of pen registers and trap-and-trace devices, physical searches, and business records for the purpose of gathering foreign intelligence.
Source: https://it.ojp.gov/default.aspx?area=privacy&page=1286
(FISC) Foreign Intelligence Surveillance Court A special court for which the Chief Justice of the United States designates 11 federal district court judges to review applications for warrants related to national security investigations.

Source: https://www.fjc.gov/history/home.nsf/page/courts_special_fisc.html
FTC Federal Trade Commission

I *Identifier/Selector* Communication accounts associated with a target (e.g., e-mails address, phone number)
IAD Information Assurance Directorate of the National Security Agency
Intelligence Community Seventeen-member group of Executive Branch agencies and organizations that work separately and together to engage in intelligence activities, either in an oversight, managerial, support, or participatory role necessary for the conduct of foreign relations and the protection of the national security of the United States.
Source: http://www.fas.org/irp/eprint/ci-glossary.pdf

M *Meta-data* A characterization or description documenting the identification, management, nature, use, or location of information resources (data).
Source: A Glossary of Archival and Records Terminology Copyright, 2012, Society of American Archivists, (http://www2.archivists.org/glossary).
(MLAT) Mutual Legal Assistance Treaty An understanding and agreement between two countries that wish to mutually cooperate regarding investigation, prosecution, and enforcement of the provisions of the laws of the agreeing countries. The MLAT also specifies the grounds on which a request by either nation may be rejected or denied by the other nation.
Source: http://perry4law.org/clic/?page_id=39

N *NAS* National Academy of Sciences
(NIPF) National Intelligence Priorities Framework DNI's guidance to the Intelligence Community on the national intelligence priorities approved by the President. The NIPF guides prioritization for the operation, planning, and programming of US intelligence analysis and collection.
Source: http://www.fbi.gov/about-us/nsb/faqs
(NSC/DC) National Security Council Deputies Committee The senior sub-Cabinet interagency forum for consideration of policy issues affecting national security. The NSC/DC prescribes and review work for the NSC interagency groups discussed in a directive. The NSC/DC helps to ensure issues brought before the NSC/PC or the NSC have been properly analyzed and prepared for decision. The regular members of the NSC/DC consist of the Deputy Secretary of State or Under Secretary of the Treasury or Under Secretary of the Treasury for International Affairs, the Deputy Secretary of Defense or Under Secretary of Defense for Policy, the Deputy Attorney General, the Deputy Director of the Office of Management and Budget, the Deputy Director of Central Intelligence, the Vice Chairman of the Joint Chiefs of Staff, the Deputy Chiefs of Staff to the President for Policy, the Chief of Staff and National Security Advisor to the Vice President, the Deputy Assistant to the President for International Economic Affairs, and the Assistant to the President and Deputy National Security Advisor (who shall serve as chair).
Source: http://www.fas.org/irp/offdocs/nspd/nspd-1.htm

(NSC/PC) National Security Council Principals Committee The senior interagency forum for consideration of policy affecting national security. The regular members of the NSC/PC consist of the Secretary of State, the Secretary of the Treasury, the Secretary of Defense, the Chief of Staff to the President, and the Assistant to the President for National Security Affairs, who serves and chair.
Source: http://www.fas.org/irp/offdocs/nspd/nspd-1.htm
(NSL) National Security Letter A letter from a United States government agency demanding information related to national security. It is independent of legal courts and therefore is different from a subpoena. It is used mainly by FBI when investigating matters related to national security. It is issued to a particular entity or organization to turn over records and data pertaining to individuals. By law, NSLs can request only non-content information, such as transactional records, phone numbers dialed, or sender or recipient of the letter from disclosing that the letter was ever issued.
Source: http://en.wikipedia.org/wiki/National_security_letter
Source: USA PATRIOT Improvement and Reauthorization Act of 2005: A legal Analysis Congressional Research Service's report for Congress, Brian T. Yeh, Charles Doyle, December 21, 2006.
NSS National Security Staff
NIST National Institute of Standards and Technology
Non-Disclosure Agreement (commonly referred to as "Gag Orders") Contracts intended to protect information considered to be proprietary or confidential. Parties involved in executing a NDA promise not to divulge secret or protected information.
Source: http://inventors.about.com/od/nondisclosure/a/Nondisclosure.htm
NRC National Research Council
NRO National Reconnaissance Office
NSA National Security Agency
NSD/DoJ National Security Division of the Department of Justice

O *ODNI* Office of the Director of National Intelligence
ODOC NSA's Office of the Director of Compliance
OIA/DoJ Office of International Affairs of the Department of Justice
OMB Office of Management and Budget
OSD Office of the Secretary of Defense
OTA Office of Technology Assessment

P *PATRIOT Act* An Act of Congress that was signed into law by President George W. Bush on October 26, 2001. The title of the act is a ten-letter acronym (USA PATRIOT) that stands for Uniting (and) Strengthening America (by) Providing Appropriate Tools Required (to) Intercept (and) Obstruct Terrorism Act of 2001.
Source:
http://www.gpo.gov/fdsys/pkg/PLAW-107publ56/html/PLAW- 107publ56.htm
PCLOB Privacy and Civil Liberties Oversight Board
Pen Register A device that decodes or records electronic impulses, allowing outgoing numbers from a telephone to be identified.
Source: http://legal-dictionary.thefreedictionary.com/Pen+Register

PII Personally identifiable information
PIBD Public Interest Declassification Board

R *(RAS) Reasonable Articulable Suspicion/Reasonable Grounds to Believe (as applied to Section 215)* A legal standard of proof in United States law that is less than probable cause, the legal standard for arrests and warrants, but more than an "inchoate and unparticularized suspicion or 'hunch'"; it must be based on "specific and articulable facts", "taken together with rational inferences from those facts."
Source: http://supreme.justia.com/cases/federal/us/392/1/case.html#27
Source: http://en.wikipedia.org/wik/Reasonable_Articulable_Suspicion#cite_ note-1
Rockefeller Commission Headed by Vice-President Nelson Rockefeller, the commission issued a single report in 1975, which delineated CIA abuses including mail openings and surveillance of domestic dissident groups.
Source: http://historymatters.com/archive/contents/church/contents_church _reports_rockcomm.htm
RSA Algorithm (Rivest-Shamir-Adleman) An Internet encryption and authentication system that uses an algorithm developed in 1977 by Ron Rivest, Adi Shamir, and Leonard Adleman. The RSA algorithm is the most commonly used encryption and authentication algorithm and is included as part of the Web browsers from Microsoft and Netscape and many other products.
Source: http://searchsecurity.techtarget.com/definition/RSA

S *Section 215* Statutory provision of FISA that permits the government access to business records for foreign intelligence and international terrorism investigations. The governing federal officials are permitted the ability to acquire business and other 'tangible records' which include: business records, phone provider records, apartment rental records, driver's license, library records, book sales records, gun sales records, tax return records, educational records, and medical records. Under this provision, federal investigators can compel third-party record holders, such as telecom firms, banks or others, to disclose these documents. In order to use this provision, the US government must show that there are reasonable grounds to believe that the records are relevant to an international terrorism or counterintelligence investigation.
Source: http://www.law.cornell.edu/uscode/text/50/1861
Source: http://belfercenter.ksg.harvard.edu/publication/19163/usapatriot_act. html
Section 702 Statutory provision for the targeting of individuals reasonably believed to be non-U.S persons located outside the United States.
Source:
http://www.fas.org/irp/news/2013/06/nsa-sect702.pdf
(SSL) Secure Sockets Layer A commonly used protocol for managing the security of a message transmission on the internet.
Source: http://searchsecurity.techtarget.com/definition/Secure-Sockets-Layer- SSL
(SIGINT) Signals Intelligence Intelligence derived from electronic signals and systems used by foreign targets, such as communications systems, and radar communications system.
Source: http://www.nsa.gov/sigint

Social Networking A dedicated website or other application that enables users to communicate with each other by posting information, comments, messages, images, etc…
Source: http://www.oxforddictionaries.com/us/definition/american_english/ social-network
Splinternet Also referred to as "cyberbalkernization" or "Internet Balkanization", it is the segregation of the Internet into smaller groups with similar interests, to a degree that they show a narrow-minded approach to outsiders or those with contradictory views.
Source: http://www.techopedia.com/definition/28087/cyberbalkanization

T *Third Party Doctrine* Provides that information "knowingly exposed" to a third party is not subject to Fourth Amendment protection because one "assumes the risk" that the third party will disclose that information. The doctrine holds that the information that individual disclosed to businesses credit card transactions, phone records, etc. doesn't carry with it a "reasonable expectation of privacy" under the Fourth Amendment, as one has "assumed the risk" that this information might at some point be disclosed.
Source: http://www.lawtechjournal.com/articles/2007/02_070426_lawless.pdf
Source: http://www.nationalreview.com/agenda/350896/third-party- doctrine-reihan-salam
T-TIP Transatlantic Trade and Investment Partnership
Trap-and-Trace A device or process that captures the incoming electronic or other impulses which identify the originating number or other dialing, routing, addressing, and signaling information reasonably likely to identify the source of a wire or electronic communication, provided, however, that such information shall not include the contents of any communication.
Source: 18 USC. § 3127(3)
Tutelage The codename of a classified NSA technology used to monitor communications used on military networks.
Source: http://www.wired.com/threatlevel/2009/07/einstein/

W *Warfighter* Military personnel with a combat or combat related mission.
Whistle-Blower A person who tells someone in authority about something they believe to be illegal that is happening, especially in a government department or a company.
Source: http://dictionary.cambridge.org/dictionary/british/whistle-blower
Wiretap To place a device on (someone's phone) in order to secretly listen to telephone calls.
Source: http://www.merriam-webster.com/dictionary/wiretap

Z *Zero Day Exploitation* Taking advantage of security vulnerability on the same day that the vulnerability becomes generally known. There are zero days between the time the vulnerability is discovered and the first attack. It is an exploit of vulnerability in software, which is being utilized for the first time and which, therefore, is unknown to defensive software.

Source: http://searchsecurity.techtarget.com/definition/zero-day-exploit

End Notes

[1] *Olmstead v. United States*, 277 US 438, 478 (Brandeis, J., dissenting).

[2] *Id.*

[3] See Frank J. Donner, *The Age of Surveillance: The Aims and Methods of America's Political Intelligence System* (Knopf 1980); Peter Irons, *Justice at War* (Oxford 1983); William H. Rehnquist, *All the Laws But One: Civil Liberties in Wartime* (Knopf 1998); James Morton Smith, *Freedom's Fetters: The Alien and Sedition Laws and American Civil Liberties* (Cornell 1956); Geoffrey R. Stone, *Perilous Times: Free Speech in Wartime from the Sedition Act of 1798 to the War on Terrorism* (W.W. Norton 2004).

[4] See *Detailed Staff Reports of the Intelligence Activities and the Rights of Americans*: Book III, Final Report of the Select Committee to Study Governmental Operations with Respect to Intelligence Activities, United States Senate, 94th (Apr. 29, 1976); Robert Justin Goldstein, *Political Repression in Modern America: From 1870 to the Present* (Schenckman 1978); Geoffrey R. Stone, *Perilous Times: Free Speech in Wartime from the Sedition Act of 1798 to the War on Terrorism*, 487-500, (W.W. Norton) 2004; Athan Theoharis, *Spying on Americans: Political Surveillance from Hoover to the Huston Plan* (Temple 1978).

[5] *See Final Report of the United States Senate Select Committee to Study Governmental Operations with Respect to Intelligence Activities*. S. Rep. No. 755, 94th Cong., 2d Sess., at 5 (April 29, 1976) (Church Committee Report).

[6] *See* Executive Order 11905, United States Foreign Intelligence Activities, 41 Fed. Reg. 7703 (Feb. 18, 1976).

[7] The Attorney General's Guidelines on Domestic Security Investigations are reprinted in FBI Domestic Security Guidelines: Oversight Hearing Before the Committee on the Judiciary, H.R., 98th Cong., 1st Sess. 67 (Apr. 27, 1983); *see also* Office of the Inspector General, Special Report: The Federal Bureau of Investigation's Compliance with the Attorney General's Investigative Guidelines ch. 2 (Sept. 2005); Geoffrey R. Stone, *Perilous Times: Free Speech in Wartime from the Sedition Act of 1798 to the War on Terrorism*, pp. 496-497 (W.W. Norton 2004).

[8] *Church Committee Report* (April 26, 1976).

[9] *Id.*, at v, vii, 1, 3.

[10] *Id.*

[11] *Id.*

[12] *Id.*

[13] *Id.*, at 4, 291-292.

[14] *Id.*

[15] *Id.*

[16] *Id.*

[17] *Id.*, at 14-15, 18, 20.

[18] *Olmstead v. United States,* 277 US 438, at 473 and 478 (1928) (Brandeis, J., dissenting).

[19] *Id.*, at 473-474 (Brandeis, J. dissenting).

[20] *Id.*, at 202.

[21] *Id.*

[22] *Id.*

[23] *Church Committee Report, (April 1976)* pp. at 290-291, quoting Robert H. Jackson, *The Supreme Court in the American System of Government,* 70-71 (New York: Harper Torchbook 1955).

[24] *Id.*, at 289 and 292.

[25] *Id.*, at 293.

[26] *Id.*, at 295-339.

[27] 50 U.S.C. ch. 36.

[28] 277 US 438 (1928).

[29] 47 U.S.C. § 151 et seq.

[30] 389 US. 347, 351 (1967).

[31] *United States v. United States District Court for the Eastern District of Michigan*, 407 US 297, 308 (1972).

[32] 124 Cong. Rev. 34,845 (1978).

[33] The Act defines "foreign power" as including, among other things, "a foreign government or any component thereof," "a faction of a foreign nation," "an entity that is openly acknowledged by a foreign government ... to be directed and controlled by such foreign government," "a group engaged in international terrorism," "a foreign-based political organization," and "an entity ... that is engaged in the international proliferation of weapons of mass destruction." 50 U.S.C. § 1801(a).

[34] 50 U.S.C. § 1805.

[35] 50 U.S.C. ch. 15.

[36] 50 U.S.C. § 3601.
[37] 50 U.S.C. § 1801.
[38] *See* 50 U.S.C. § 1842 (2008) (pen register and trap- and- trace); 50 U.S.C. § 1862(a) (2001) (business records).
[39] 50 U.S.C. ch. 15.
[40] 50 U.S.C. § 403a.
[41] 50 U.S.C. § 3601.
[42] 5 U.S.C. § 552(a).
[43] 18 U.S.C. §§ 2510–2522.
[44] Exec. Order No. 12333, 40 Fed. Reg. 235 (December 4, 1981), as amended by Executive Order 13284 (Jan. 23, 2003), and by Executive Order 13355 (Aug. 27, 2004), and further amended by Executive Order 13470 (July 30, 2008). Executive Order 12333 was first issued by President Gerald Ford as Executive Order 11905 and then replaced by President Jimmy Carter as Executive Order 12036, the current *United States Intelligence Activities* was signed on December 4, 1981 as Executive Order 12333 by President Ronald Reagan and updated by President George W. Bush in 2008.
[45] These Guidelines are captured in the Department of Defense Directive 5240.1-R entitled, "DOD Activities that May Affect US Persons," including a classified appendix particularized for NSA. The guidelines are further enunciated within NSA through an internal directive, US Signals Intelligence Directive 18, commonly referred to as USSID-18.
[46] Jack Goldsmith, *The Terror Presidency: Law and Judgment Inside the Bush Administration* pp. 73-74 (W.W. Norton 2007).
[47] *Id.*
[48] Executive Order 12333 § 2.1.
[49] Minimization procedures govern the implementation of electronic surveillance to ensure that it conforms to its authorized purpose and scope. They require the government to "minimize" the retention and dissemination of US person information acquired by inadvertent collection. Under FISA, minimization procedures are adopted by the Attorney General and reviewed by the FISA Court. *See* 50 U.S.C.A. § 1801(h). *See* generally David S. Kris and J. Douglas Wilson, I *National Security Investigations and Prosecutions 2d* pp. 321-353 (West 2012).
[50] *See* Uniting and Strengthening America by Providing Appropriate Tools Required to Intercept and Obstruct Terrorism ("USA PATRIOT Act") Act of 2001, Pub. L. 107-56, § 215, 115 Stat. 272, 287 (2001) (codified as amended at 50 U.S.C. § 1861(a)(1)) (2006 & Supp. V 2011).
[51] Intelligence Authorization Act for Fiscal Year 1999, Pub. L. 105-272, § 602, 112 Stat. 2396, 2410 (1998).
[52] *Id.*
[53] *See* Uniting and Strengthening America by Providing Appropriate Tools Required to Intercept and Obstruct Terrorism ("USA PATRIOT Act") Act of 2001, Pub. L. 107-56, § 215, 115 Stat. 272, 287 (2001) (codified as amended at 50 U.S.C. § 1861(a)(1)) (2006 & Supp. V 2011).
[54] USA PATRIOT Improvement and Reauthorization Act of 2005 § 106, 120 Stat. 196 (codified as amended at 50 U.S.C. § 1861(b)(2)(A)). Section 215 provides that such investigations of United States persons may not be "conducted solely on the basis of activities protected by the first amendment to the Constitution." For certain materials, such as library records, book sales records, firearms sales records, tax return records, educational records, and medical records with information identifying an individual, only the Director of the FBI, the Deputy Director of the FBI, or the Executive Assistant for National Security may make the application. *See* 50 U.S.C. § 1863(a)(3) (2006).
[55] *Hale v. Henkel*, 201 US 43, 76 (1906).
[56] 425 US 435 (1976).
[57] 442 US 735 (1979).
[58] Section 1114, Pub. L. 95-630, 92 Stat. 3706 (1978).
[59] *Id.*
[60] 50 U.S.C. § 1842.
[61] *Id.* This is similar to the authority federal law grants to federal and state prosecutors and local police officials to obtain court orders for the installation of pen registers and trap-and-trace devices upon certification that the information sought is relevant to an ongoing criminal investigation. See 18 U.S.C. § 3122.
[62] 50 U.S.C. § 1861(a)(1).
[63] *See* 115 Stat. § 288-291 (2001).
[64] 132 S.Ct. 945 (2012).
[65] *Id.*, at 957 (Sotomayor, J., concurring).
[66] *Id.*, at 950 (Alito, J., concurring), quoting *Kyllo v. United States*, 533 US 27, 34 (2001).
[67] *Id.*, at 964 (Alito, J., concurring).
[68] *See* 50 U.S.C. § 1861(b)(2)(A). Section 215 provides that such investigations of United States persons may not be "conducted solely on the basis of activities protected by the first amendment to the Constitution."
[69] 50 U.S.C. § 1861(c)(2)(D).
[70] *California v. Acevedo*, 500 US 565, 568 (1991). (quoting *Johnson v. United States,* 333 U.S. 10, 14 (1948).

[71] Administrative subpoenas are authorized by many federal statutes and may be issued by most federal agencies. Most statutes authorizing administrative subpoenas authorize an agency to require the production of certain records for civil rather than criminal matters.

[72] 12 U.S.C. § 3414, 15 U.S.C. § 1681(u), 15 U.S.C. § 1681(v), 18 U.S.C. § 2709, and 50 U.S.C. § 436.

[73] 50 U.S.C. § 1801.

[74] Pub. L. 107-56, 115 Stat. 365 (2001).

[75] *See* 18 U.S.C. § 3511.

[76] It should be noted that there are at least two distinctions between NSLs and federal grand jury subpoenas. First, where the FBI believes that records should be sought, it can act directly by issuing NSLs, but to obtain a grand jury subpoena the FBI must obtain approval by a prosecutor at the Department of Justice. Second, and except in exceptional circumstances, witnesses who appear before a grand jury ordinarily are not under nondisclosure orders preventing them from stating that they have been called as witnesses.

[77] *See* David S. Kris and J. Douglas Wilson, I *National Security Investigations and Prosecutions 2d,* pp. 727-763 (West 2012).

[78] *See* Department of Justice, Office of the inspector General, A Review of the Federal Bureau of Investigation's Use of National Security Letters (Unclassified) (March 2007). *Note: Subsequent reports from the IG have noted the FBI and DOJ have resolved many of the compliance incidents.*

[79] United States Department of Justice, Office of the Inspector General, *A Review of the FBI's Use of Section 215 Orders for Business Records in 2006* 5 (March 2008), quoted in Kris & Wilson, *National Security Investigations and Prosecutions* at 748. In recent years, the FBI has put in place procedures to reduce the risk of noncompliance.

[80] 18 U.S.C. § 1861(g).

[81] In *Doe v. Mukasey*, 549 F.3d 861 (2d Cir. 2008), the court held that the FBI's use of nondisclosure orders violated the First Amendment. In response, the FBI amended its procedures to provide that if a recipient of an NSL objects to a non-disclosure order, the FBI must obtain a court order based on a demonstrated need for secrecy in order for it to enforce the non-disclosure order.

[82] 18 U.S.C. app. 3 §§ 1-16.

[83] It is essential that the standards and processes for issuance of NSLs match as closely as possible the standards and processes for issuance of section 215 orders. Otherwise, the FBI will naturally opt to use NSLs whenever possible in order to circumvent the more demanding – and perfectly appropriate – section 215 standards. We reiterate that if judicial orders are required for the issuance of NSLs, there should be an exception for emergency situations when time is of the essence.

[84] *See In re Application of the Federal Bureau of Investigation for an Order Requiring the Prod. Of Tangible Things from [Telecommunications Providers] Relating to [Redacted version]*, Order No. BR-05 (FISC May 24, 2006).

[85] *In re Application of the Federal Bureau of Investigation for an Order Requiring the Production of Tangible Things from [Undisclosed Service Provider]*, Docket Number: BR 13-109 (FISC Oct. 11, 2013) (hereinafter FISC order 10/11/2013).

[86] *Id.*

[87] *Id.*

[88] *Id.*

[89] *In Re Production of Tangible Things from [Undisclosed Service Provider]*, Docket Number: BR-08-13 (FISC Dec. 12, 2008), quoting Application Exhibit A, Declaration of [Redacted version] (Dec. 11, 2008).

[90] Administration White Paper, *Bulk Collection of Telephony Meta-data Under Section 215 of the USA PATRIOT Act,* at 3-4 (August 9, 2013).

[91] For several years, NSA used a similar meta-data program for Internet communications under the authority of FISA's pen register and trap-and-trace provisions rather than under the authority of section 215. NSA suspended this e-mail meta-data program in 2009 because of compliance issues (it came to light that NSA had inadvertently been collecting certain types of information that were not consistent with the FISC's authorization orders). After re-starting it in 2010, NSA Director General Keith Alexander decided to let the program expire at the end of 2011 because, for operational and technical reasons, the program was insufficiently productive to justify the cost. The possibility of revising and reinstituting such a program was left open, however. This program posed problems similar to those posed by the section 215 program, and any effort to re-initiate such a program should be governed by the same recommendations we make with respect to the section 215 program.

[92] Appropriately trained and authorized technical personnel may also access the meta-data "to perform those processes needed to make it usable for intelligence analysis," and for related technical purposes, according to the FISC orders.

[93] 50 U.S.C. 1801(i). A "United States person" is either a citizen of the United States or a non-citizen who is a legal permanent resident of the United States.

[94] *In Re Application of the Federal Bureau of Investigation for an Order Requiring the Production of Tangible Things from [Undisclosed Service Provider],* Docket Number: BR 13-158 (FISC, Dec. 2011).

[95] *Id.*, at 14.
[96] *Id.*, at 14-15.
[97] *Id.*, at 15.
[98] *In re Application of the Federal Bureau of Investigation for an Order Requiring the Production of Tangible Things from [Undisclosed Service Provider]*, Docket Number: BR 13-109 (FISC Oct. 11, 2013) (hereinafter FISC order 10/11/2013).
[99] *In Re Production of Tangible Things From [Undisclosed Service Provider*, Docket Number: BR 08-13 (March 2, 2009).
[100] *Id.*
[101] *Id.*
[102] *Id.*
[103] *Id.*
[104] *Id.*
[105] *See In re Production of Tangible Things From [Redacted version*], No. BR-09-13 (FISC, September 3, 2009).
[106] *Id.*
[107] *In Re Application of the Federal Bureau of Investigation for an Order Requiring the Production of Tangible Things From [Redacted version]*, Docket No. BR 13-158 (FISC Oct. 11, 2013), pp. 5-6.
[108] David S. Kris, *On the Bulk Collection of Tangible Things*, 1 Lawfare Research Paper Series 4 at 26 (Sept. 29, 2013).
[109] *In Re Application of the Federal Bureau of Investigation for an Order Requiring the Production of Tangible Things From [Redacted version]*, Docket No. BR 13-109 (FISC Aug. 29, 2013).
[110] *See* Kris, *On the Bulk Collection of Tangible Things,* p. 34. Indeed, the government has suggested that "communications meta-data is different from many other kinds of records because it is inter-connected and the connections between individual data points, which can be reliably identified only through analysis of a large volume of data, are particularly important to a broad range of investigations of international terrorism." *Administration White Paper,* p. 2.
[111] National Research Council of the National Academy of Science, *Protecting Individual Privacy in the Struggle Against Terrorists: A Framework for Program Assessment,* pp. 2-3 (National Academies Press 2008).
[112] *Id.*
[113] *Church Committee Report* at 778 (April 1976).
[114] It is possible, of course, for the government carefully to target its collection and retention of data in a way that maximizes the benefit and minimizes the cost, thereby substantially altering the balance of costs and benefits. But there is no reason to believe that this describes the decision to collect bulk telephony meta-data, in particular.
[115] *United States v. Jones,* 132 S.Ct. 945, 955 (2012) (Sotomayor, J., concurring).
[116] *Id.*
[117] *Id.* at 956 (Sotomayor, J., concurring) (quoting *United States v. Cuevas-Perez,* 640 F.3d 272, 285 (C.A. 7, 2011) (Flaum, J., concurring).
[118] For example, Congress might enact legislation requiring relevant telephone providers to retain the data for a specified period of time to ensure that it will be available if and when the government needs to query it. In that case, the government should reimburse the providers for the cost of retaining the data. Based on our review, an appropriate period of time would seem to be no more than two years. A Federal Commnications Commission (FCC) regulation already requires providers to hold such information for 18 months, so it seems feasible to change the retention period for telephone records. The FCC's rule on retention of telephone toll records is 47 C.F.R. § 42.6: "Retention of telephone toll records. Each carrier that offers or bills toll telephone service shall retain for a period of 18 months such records as are necessary to provide the following billing information about telephone toll calls: the name, address, and telephone number of the caller, telephone number called, date, time, and length of the call. Each carrier shall retain this information for toll calls that it bills whether it is billing its own toll service customers for toll calls or billing customers for another carrier. 60 Fed. Reg. 2d 1529 (1986); 51 FR 32651, corrected, 51 FR 39536.
[119] It is noteworthy that the section 215 telephony meta-data program has made only a modest contribution to the nation's security. It is useful to compare it, for example, to the section 702 program, which we discuss in the next Part of our Report. Whereas collection under section 702 has produced significant information in many, perhaps most, of the 54 situations in which signals intelligence has contributed to the prevention of terrorist attacks since 2007, section 215 has generated relevant information in only a small number of cases, and there has been no instance in which NSA could say with confidence that the outcome would have been different without the section 215 telephony meta-data program. Moreover, now that the existence of the program has been disclosed publicly, we suspect that it is likely to be less useful still.
[120] See *International Principles on the Application of Human Rights to Communications Surveillance*, 10 July 2013, available at http://en.necessaryandproportionate.org/text.
[121] 442 US 735 (1979).

[122] Letter from James Madison to W.T. Barry (Aug. 4, 1822) in *The Writings of James Madison* at 103 (Gaillard Hunt, ed., G.P. Putnam's Sons) 1910.

[123] Public Interest Declassification Board, *Transforming the Security Classification System*, 1-2 (2012), pp.1-2.

[124] On October 10, 2012, President Obama issued Presidential Policy Directive/PPD-19, which prohibits any retaliatory employment action against any government employee with access to classified information who reports any instance of "waste, fraud, and abuse," including violations "of any law, rule, or regulation," to "a supervisor in the employee's direct chain of command up to and including the head of the employing agency, to the Inspector General of the employing agency or Intelligence Community Element, to the Director of National Intelligence, to the Inspector General of the Intelligence Community." *Id.* Although this is an important step in the right direction, it does not go far enough. First, it covers only government employees and not government contractors. Second, it requires the would-be whistle-blower to report to a person in his "direct chain of command," rather than to an independent authority. We discuss whistle-blowing in Chaper VI.

[125] Similarly, in the context of the non-disclosure orders addressed in Recommendation 9, the government should be able to act without prior judicial authority in cases of emergency.

[126] The Universal Declaration of Human Rights, Art. 12 states, "No one shall be subjected to arbitrary interference with his privacy…"

[127] *See* 18 U.S.C. § 2518(3).

[128] H. Rep. No. 95-1283 (I) at 50-51 (June 5, 1978).

[129] Executive Order 12333, which governs the use of electronic surveillance by the Intelligence Community outside the United States, provides that "timely, accurate, and insightful information about the activities, capabilities, plans, and intentions of foreign powers, organizations, persons, and their agents, is essential to the national security of the United States." It declares that "special emphasis should be given to detecting and countering" espionage, terrorism, and the development, possession, proliferation, or use of weapons of mass destruction. The executive order directs that "such techniques as electronic surveillance" may not be used "unless they are in accordance with procedures ... approved by the Attorney General" and that "such procedures shall protect constitutional and other legal rights and limit use of such information to lawful governmental purposes."

[130] The Protect America Act of 2007, Pub. L. 111-55 (Aug. 5, 2007) which amended 50 U.S.C. § 1803 et. seq., by adding §§ 1803 a-c.

[131] *See* 50 U.S.C. § 1881(c).

[132] *See* 50 U.S.C. § 1881(a).

[133] *See* 50 U.S.C. §1881. Service providers who are subject to these orders are entitled to compensation and are immune from suit for their assistance. They may petition the FISC to set aside or modify the directive if they think that it is unlawful. If a provider is uncooperative, the Attorney General may petition the FISC for an order to enforce the directive.

[134] *See generally* 50 U.S.C. 1881a.

[135] *Id.*

[136] S. Rep. 112-174 (June 7, 2012).

[137] The term "upstream collection" refers to NSA's interception of Internet communications as they transit the facilities of an Internet backbone carrier.

[138] MCTs arise in situations in which many communications are bundled together within a single Internet transmission and when the lawful interception of one communication in the bundle results in the interception of them all.

[139] *In Re DNI/AG 702(g)*, Docket Number 702(i)-11-01 (FISC October 3, 2011) (hereinafter cited as FISC Oct. 3, 2011 opinion).

[140] *Id.*

[141] *Id.*

[142] *Id.*

[143] *Id.*

[144] *In re DNI/AG 702(g)*, Docket Number 702(i)-11-01 (FISC November 30, 2011) (Redacted version).

[145] National Security Agency, *The National Security Agency: Missions, Authorities, Oveersight and Partnerships* (August 9, 2013).

[146] Background Paper on Title VII of FISA Prepared by the Department of Justice and the Office of the Director of National Intelligence (ODNI), Appendix to Senate Select Committee on Intelligence, *Report on FAA Sunsets Extension Act of 2012*, 112th Congress, Cong., 2d Session (June 7, 2012).

[147] Senate Select Committee on Intelligence, *Report on FAA Sunsets Extension Act of 2012*, 112th Congress, 2d Session (June 7, 2012).

[148] 28 C.F.R. ch. I, Part 23.

[149] NSA's Section 702 Minimization Procedures.

[150] Recommendation 12(2) is designed to address this latter concern. If the government cannot use the evidence in any legal proceeding against the US person, it is less likely to use section 702 in an effort to obtain such information. On the other hand, we do not recommend prohibiting the use of the "fruits" of such interceptions. We draw the line as we do because, unlike most "fruit of the poisonous tree" situations, the interception in this

situation is not itself unlawful unless it was *actually* motivated by a desire to obtain information about the US person.

[151] Although the Supreme Court has never directly addressed this question, "every court of appeals to have considered the question" has held "that the Fourth Amendment applies to searches conducted by the United States Government against United States citizens abroad." *United States v. Verdugo-Urquidez*, 494 US 259, 283 n.7 (1990) (Brennan, J., dissenting). See *In re Terrorist Bombings of US. Embassies in East Africa*, 552 F.3d 157 (2010); *United States v. Bin Laden*, 126 F. Supp. 2d 264, 270-271 (S.D.N.Y. 2000), aff'd, 552 F.3d 157 (2d Cir. 2008); David S. Kris & J. Douglas Wilson, I, *National Security Investigations and Prosecutions 2d* at 596-597 (West 2012).

[152] See *United States v. Verdugo-Urquidez*, 494 US. 259, 265-266 (1990). Noting that the Fourth Amendment protects the right of "the people," the Court held that this "refers to a class of persons who are part of a national community or who have otherwise developed sufficient connection with this country to be considered part of that community."

[153] It is important to note that although the government should not target a non-US person outside the United States for surveillance *solely* because of his political or religious activity or expression, it may target such an individual for surveillance if it has reason to believe that he poses a threat to US national security.

[154] 5 U.S.C. § 552(a).

[155] Department of Homeland Security: Privacy Policy Guidance Memorandum No. 2007-1 (January 7, 2007) (amended on January 19, 2007).

[156] *Id.*

[157] *Id.*

[158] 44 U.S.C. § 101.

[159] Potential Changes to the Foreign Intelligence Surveillance Act: Open Hearing Before the H.P. Select Comm. on Intelligence, 113 Cong. (October 29, 2013) (Statement of James R. Clapper, Director of National Intelligence).

[160] *See* Jonathan Mayer, "The Web is Flat" Oct. 30, 2013 (study showing "pervasive" flow of web browsing data outside of the US for US individuals using US-based websites), available at http://webpolicy.org/2013/10/30/the-web-is-flat/.

[161] Susan Landau, *Surveillance or Security: The Risks Posed by New Wiretapping Technologies* (MIT Press 2011); Jon M. Peha, *The Dangerous Policy of Weakening Security to Facilitate Surveillance*, Oct. 4, 2013, available at http://ssrn.com/abstract=2350929.

[162] Although DHS was created ten years ago, Congress has yet to readjust its committees of jurisdiction.

[163] See Peter Swire, "The Administration Response to the Challenges of Protecting Privacy," Jan. 8, 2000, available at www.peterswire.net/pubs. Peter Swire is one of the five members of the Review Group; the comments in text are made here on behalf of the entire Review Group.

[164] In one instance, the FISC heard arguments from a non-governmental party that sought to contest a directive from the government. In 2007, Yahoo declined to comply with a directive from the government. The government then filed a motion with the FISC to compel compliance. The FISC received briefings from both Yahoo and the government, and then rendered its decision in 2008 in favor of the government. Yahoo then appealed unsuccessfully to the FISA Court of Review. *See In re Directives [Redacted Version] Pursuant to Section 105b of the Foreign Intelligence Surveillance Act*, 551 F.3d 1004 (FISA Ct. Rev. 2008). In several other instances, private parties, including the American Civil Liberties Union and the Electronic Frontier Foundation, Google, Inc., Microsoft Corporation, and the Media Freedom and Information Access Clinic, filed motions with the FISC seeking the release or disclosure of certain records. See Letter from Chief Judge Reggie Walton to Honorable Patrick Leahy (July 29, 2013); *In re Motion for Release of Court Records,* 526 F. Supp. 484 (FISA Ct. 2007).

[165] Letter from Chief Judge Reggie Walton to Honorable Patrick Leahy (July 29, 2013).

[166] Other possible institutional homes for the Advocate appear to have serious shortcomings. Housing the Public Advocate with the FISC would run the risk of the Advocate often having little or nothing to do. Housing the Advocate within the Department of Justice would undermine the independence of the Advocate from the opposing brief writers in the case, who would also be in the same Department. Using a rotating panel of outside lawyers would risk a loss of continuity and knowledge about classified programs.

[167] "FISA Files" are files relating to the Foreign Intelligence Surveillance Act (FISA). These "FISA Files" may include the following: a request to initiate collection activity; an application; court order or authorization by the Attorney General; draft documents; related memoranda; motions, affidavits, filings, correspondence, and electronic communications; and other related documents or records. See p. 8 of United States Department of Justice "Automatic Declassification Guide — FOR USE AND REVIEW AND DECLASSIFICATION OF RECORDS UNDER EXECUTIVE ORDER 13526, "CLASSIFIED NATIONAL SECURITY INFORMATION."

[168] Louis Brandeis, *Other People's Money – And How Bankers Use It*, Chapter 5 (1914).

[169] White House Fact Sheet: *Transatlantic Trade and Investment Partnership (T-TIP)*, June, 2013, available at http://www.ustr.gov/about-us/press-office/fact-sheets/2013/june/wh-ttip.

170 "Draft Working Document on Foreign Policy Aspect of the Inquiry on Electronic Mass Surveillance of EU Citizens," European Parliament Committee on Foreign Affairs, Nov. 4, 2013, available at http://www.statewatch.org/news/2013/nov/ep-nsa-surv-inq-working-document-fa-committee.pdf.

171 "Bhatt Jaheen, "In Wake of PRISM, German DPAs Threaten to Halt Data Transfers to Non-EU Countries," Bloomberg BNA, July 29, 2013, available at http://www.bna.com/wake-prism- germann17179875O2.

172 "Garner Predict Cloud Computing Spending to Increase by 100% in 2016, says AppsCare," PRWEb.com, 2012, available at http://prweb.com/releases/2012/7/prweb9711167.htm.

173 Daniel Castro, "How Much Will PRISM Cost the US Cloud Computing Industry," August, 2013 (estimating monetary impact on US cloud providers of $21.5 billion by 2016, based on 10% loss in foreign market share), available at www2.itif.org/2013-cloud-computing-costs.pdf; Cloud Security Alliance, "CSA Survey Results: Government Access to Information", July 2013, available at https://downloads.cloudsecurityalliance.org/ initiatives/surveys/nsa_prism/CSA-govt-access-survey- July-2013.pdf (losses up to $180 billion by 2016).

174 Any cryptographic algorithm can become exploitable if implemented incorrectly or used improperly.

175 We should emphasize here that data- mining and big data have been the subject of previous federally - funded reports, notably including "Safeguarding Privacy in the Fight Against Terrorism," from the Technology and Privacy Advisory Committee of the Department of Defense (2004), and "Protecting Individual Privacy in the Struggle Against Terrorists: A Framework for Program Assessment," by the National Research Council (2008). These studies, have examined issues of data- mining in considerable detail, and we have found them useful and illuminating. Related academic work includes Fred H. Cate, "Government Data Mining: the Need for a Legal Framework," Harvard Civil Rights-Civil Liberties Law Review 43, 2008; Peter Swire, "Privacy and Information Sharing in the War Against Terrorism," 51 Villanova Law Review 260, 2006. We encourage agencies to study this literature, and adopt risk management approaches where feasible.

176 The Federal Trade Commission (FTC) often plays this role for evolving privacy-related issues, such as through its recent workshops on the Internet of Things or Big Data. The FTC's jurisdiction, however, is limited to the commercial sector. It has no jurisdiction over technology issues facing government agencies, including the Intelligence Community.

177 If an OTA is not created within the PCLOB or a new CLPP Board, then the intelligence community should find other mechanisms to institutionalize the effects of new programs on privacy, civil liberties, and the other important values implicated by cutting-edge intelligence technologies. These new mechanisms must include effective participation by expert technologists beyond those involved in development of the program.

178 Office of Director of National Intelligence, *2012 Report on Security Clearance Determinations*, p. 3, Table 1, (January 2013) available at www.fas.org/sgp/othergov/intel/clear-2012.pdf.

179 Office of Director of National Intelligence, *2012 Report on Security Clearance Determinations*, p. 7, Table 5, (January 2013) available at www.fas.org/sgp/othergov/intel/clear-2012.pdf.

180 Michael Morell affirmatively recused himself from Review Group discussions of network security to mitigate the insider threat due to ongoing business interests.

181 See OMB Circular A-4.

182 This paper addresses the strength of standard cryptographic algorithms. Any cryptographic algorithm can become exploitable if implemented incorrectly or used improperly. NSA works with NIST to ensure that NIST standards incorporate guidance on correct implementation and usage. NSA will exploit vulnerable implementations and uses to support the lawful conduct of signals intelligence.

In: Balancing Liberty, Privacy, and Security ...
Editor: Benji Norwood

ISBN: 978-1-63117-999-0

Chapter 2

FACT SHEET: REVIEW OF U.S. SIGNALS INTELLIGENCE*

Office of the Press Secretary

ABSTRACT

In the latter half of 2013 and early 2014, the United States Government undertook a broad-ranging and unprecedented review of our signals intelligence programs, led by the White House with relevant Departments and Agencies across the Government. In addition to our own intensive work, the review process drew on input from key stakeholders, including Congress, the tech community, civil society, foreign partners, the Review Group on Intelligence and Communication Technologies, the Privacy and Civil Liberties Oversight Board, and others. The Administration's review examined how, in light of new and changing technologies, we can use our intelligence capabilities in a way that optimally protects our national security while supporting our foreign policy, respecting privacy and civil liberties, maintaining the public trust, and reducing the risk of unauthorized disclosures. On January 17, 2014, the President delivered a speech at the Department of Justice to announce the outcomes of this review process.

In that speech, the President made clear that the men and women of the U.S. intelligence community, including the NSA, consistently follow those protocols designed to protect the privacy of ordinary people and are not abusing authorities. When mistakes have been made, they have corrected those mistakes. But for our intelligence community to be effective over the long haul, we must maintain the trust of the American people, and people around the world. To that end, the Administration has developed a path forward that we believe should give the American people greater confidence that their rights are being protected, while preserving important tools that keep us safe, and that addresses significant questions that have been raised overseas. Today the President announced the Administration's adoption of a series of concrete and substantial reforms that the Administration will adopt administratively or seek to codify with Congress, to include a majority of the recommendations.

NEW PRESIDENTIAL POLICY DIRECTIVE

* This is an edited, reformatted and augmented version of a document released by the White House, January 17, 2014.

Today, President Obama issued a new presidential policy for our signals intelligence activities, at home and abroad. This directive lays out new principles that govern how we conduct signals intelligence collection, and strengthen how we provide executive branch oversight of our signals intelligence activities. It will ensure that we take into account our security requirements, but also our alliances; our trade and investment relationships, including the concerns of our companies; and our commitment to privacy and basic liberties. And we will review decisions about intelligence priorities and sensitive targets on an annual basis, so that our actions are regularly scrutinized by the President's senior national security team.

THE FOREIGN INTELLIGENCE SURVEILLANCE COURT (FISC)

Since the review began, we've declassified over 40 opinions and orders of the Foreign Intelligence Surveillance Court, which provides judicial review of some of our most sensitive intelligence activities – including the Section 702 program targeting foreign individuals overseas and the Section 215 telephone metadata program. Going forward, the President directed the Director of National Intelligence, in consultation with the Attorney General, to annually review – for the purpose of declassification – any future opinions of the Court with broad privacy implications, and to report to the President and Congress on these efforts. To ensure that the Court hears a broader range of privacy perspectives, the President called on Congress to authorize the establishment of a panel of advocates from outside the government to provide an independent voice in significant cases before the Court.

SECTION 702 OF FOREIGN INTELLIGENCE SURVEILLANCE ACT

Section 702 is a valuable program that allows the government to intercept the communications of foreign targets overseas who have information that's important to our national security. The President believes that we can do more to ensure that the civil liberties of U.S. persons are not compromised in this program. To address incidental collection of communications between Americans and foreign citizens, the President has asked the Attorney General and DNI to initiate reforms that place additional restrictions on the government's ability to retain, search, and use in criminal cases, communications between Americans and foreign citizens incidentally collected under Section 702.

SECTION 215 OF THE PATRIOT ACT

Under Section 215 of the PATRIOT Act the government collects meta-data related to telephone calls in bulk. We believe this is a capability that we must preserve, and would note that the Review Group turned up no indication that the program had been intentionally abused. But, we believe we must do more to give people confidence. For this reason, the President ordered a transition that will end the Section 215 bulk metadata program as it currently exists, and establish a program that preserves the capabilities we need without the government holding the data.

This transition has two steps. Effective immediately, we will only pursue phone calls that are two steps removed from a number associated with a terrorist organization instead of three. The President has directed the Attorney General to work with the Foreign Intelligence Surveillance Court so that during this transition period, the database can be queried only after a judicial finding, or in a true emergency. On the broader question, the President has instructed the intelligence community and the Attorney General to use this transition period to develop options for a new program that can match the capabilities and fill the gaps that the Section 215 program was designed to address without the government holding this meta-data, and report back to him with options for alternative approaches before the program comes up for reauthorization on March 28. At the same time, the President will consult with the relevant committees in Congress to seek their views, and then seek congressional authorization for the new program as needed.

NATIONAL SECURITY LETTERS

In investigating threats, the FBI relies on the use of National Security Letters (NSLs), which can be used to require companies to provide certain types of information to the government without disclosing the orders to the subject of the investigation. In order to be more transparent in how the government uses this authority, the President directed the Attorney General to amend how we use NSLs to ensure that non-disclosure is not indefinite, and will terminate within a fixed time unless the government demonstrates a need for further secrecy.

We will also enable communications providers to make public more information than ever before about the orders they have received to provide data to the government. These companies have made clear that they want to be more transparent about the FISA, NSL and law enforcement requests that they receive from the government. The Administration agrees that these concerns are important, and is in discussions with the providers about ways in which additional information could be made public.

INCREASING CONFIDENCE OVERSEAS

U.S. global leadership demands that we balance our security requirements against our need to maintain trust and cooperation among people and leaders around the world. For that reason, the new presidential guidance lays out principles that govern what we do abroad, and clarifies what we don't do. The United States only uses signals intelligence for legitimate national security purposes, and not for the purpose of indiscriminately reviewing the e-mails or phone calls of ordinary people.

What we don't do: The United States does not collect intelligence to suppress criticism or dissent. We do not collect intelligence to disadvantage people based on their ethnicity, race, gender, sexual orientation, or religion. And we do not collect intelligence to provide a competitive advantage to U.S. companies, or U.S. commercial sectors.

What we will do: In terms of our bulk collection, we will only use data to meet specific security requirements: counter-intelligence; counter-terrorism; counter-proliferation; cybersecurity; force protection for our troops and allies; and combating transnational crime, including sanctions evasion.

The President has also decided that we will take the unprecedented step of extending certain protections that we have for the American people to people overseas. He has directed the Attorney General and DNI to develop these safeguards, which will limit the duration that we can hold personal information, while also restricting the dissemination of this information.

People around the world – regardless of their nationality – should know that the United States is not spying on ordinary people who don't threaten our national security and takes their privacy concerns into account.

This applies to foreign leaders as well. Given the understandable attention that this issue has received, the President has made clear to the intelligence community that – unless there is a compelling national security purpose – we will not monitor the communications of heads of state and government of our close friends and allies. And he has instructed his national security team, as well as the intelligence community, to work with foreign counterparts to deepen our coordination and cooperation in ways that rebuild trust going forward.

While our intelligence agencies will continue to gather information about the intentions of governments – as opposed to ordinary citizens – around the world, in the same way that the intelligence services of every other nation do, we will not apologize because our services may be more effective. But heads of state and government with whom we work closely, on whose cooperation we depend, should feel confident that we are treating them as real partners. The changes the President ordered do just that.

INTERNATIONAL ENGAGEMENT

To support our work, the President has directed changes to how our government is organized. The State Department will designate a senior officer to coordinate our diplomacy on issues related to technology and signals intelligence. The Administration will appoint a senior official at the White House to implement the new privacy safeguards that we have announced today. And the President has also asked his Counselor, John Podesta, to lead a review of big data and privacy. This group will consist of government officials who—along with the President's Council of Advisors on Science and Technology—will reach out to privacy experts, technologists and business leaders, and look at how the challenges inherent in big data are being confronted by both the public and private sectors; whether we can forge international norms on how to manage this data; and how we can continue to promote the free flow of information in ways that are consistent with both privacy and security.

The President also announced that we will devote resources to centralize and improve the process we use to handle foreign requests for legal assistance, called the Mutual Legal Assistance Treaty (MLAT) process. Under MLAT, foreign partners can request access to information stored in the United States pursuant to U.S. law. As the concentration of U.S.-based cloud storage providers has increased, so has the number of MLAT requests. To address this increase, we will speed up and centralize MLAT processing; we will implement new technology to increase the efficiency and transparency of the process; and we will increase our international outreach and training to help ensure that requests meet U.S. legal standards. We will put the necessary resources in place to reduce our response time by half by the end of 2015, and we will work aggressively to respond to legally sufficient requests in a matter of weeks. This change will ensure that our foreign partners can more effectively use information held in the U.S. to prosecute terrorists and other criminals, while still meeting the strict privacy protections put in place by U.S. law.

***

In addition to the initiatives that were announced by the President, the Administration's review affirmed our commitment to ongoing initiatives:

CONSUMER PRIVACY CODES OF CONDUCT

Two years ago, the President released a Blueprint for Consumer Privacy in the Digital Age as a "dynamic model of how to offer strong privacy protection and enable ongoing innovation in new information technologies." Following the release of the Blueprint, the Administration has convened the private sector, privacy experts, and consumer advocates to develop voluntary codes of conduct to safeguard sensitive consumer data. Last summer a multi-stakeholder group completed the first such code on how mobile apps should access private information. The Department of Commerce is continuing this multi-stakeholder process, aiming to launch the development of new codes of conduct in 2014.

COMMITMENT TO AN OPEN INTERNET

Maintaining an open, accessible Internet, including the ability to transmit data across borders freely is essential for global growth and development. We will redouble our commitment to promote the free-flow of information around the world through an inclusive approach to Internet governance and policymaking. Individuals in the 21st century depend on free and unfettered access to data flows without arbitrary government regulation. Businesses depend increasingly on agreed data-sharing regimes that allow information to move seamlessly across borders in support of global business operations. Developing countries and small businesses around the world in particular have a lot at stake, and much to lose from limitations restricting the Internet as an engine of prosperity and expression. Requirements to store data or locate hardware in a given location hurt competition, stifle innovation, and diminish economic growth. And they undermine the DNA of the Internet, which by design is a globally-distributed network of networks. We will continue to support the multi-stakeholder, inclusive approach to the Internet and work to strengthen and make more inclusive its policy-making, standards-setting, and governance organizations.

In: Balancing Liberty, Privacy, and Security …
Editor: Benji Norwood
ISBN: 978-1-63117-999-0

Chapter 3

PRESIDENTIAL POLICY DIRECTIVE/PPD-28: SIGNALS INTELLIGENCE ACTIVITIES*

Office of the Press Secretary

The United States, like other nations, has gathered intelligence throughout its history to ensure that national security and foreign policy decisionmakers have access to timely, accurate, and insightful information.

The collection of signals intelligence is necessary for the United States to advance its national security and foreign policy interests and to protect its citizens and the citizens of its allies and partners from harm. At the same time, signals intelligence activities and the possibility that such activities may be improperly disclosed to the public pose multiple risks. These include risks to: our relationships with other nations, including the cooperation we receive from other nations on law enforcement, counterterrorism, and other issues; our commercial, economic, and financial interests, including a potential loss of international trust in U.S. firms and the decreased willingness of other nations to participate in international data sharing, privacy, and regulatory regimes; the credibility of our commitment to an open, interoperable, and secure global Internet; and the protection of intelligence sources and methods.

In addition, our signals intelligence activities must take into account that all persons should be treated with dignity and respect, regardless of their nationality or wherever they might reside, and that all persons have legitimate privacy interests in the handling of their personal information.

In determining why, whether, when, and how the United States conducts signals intelligence activities, we must weigh all of these considerations in a context in which information and communications technologies are constantly changing. The evolution of technology has created a world where communications important to our national security and the communications all of us make as part of our daily lives are transmitted through the same channels. This presents new and diverse opportunities for, and challenges with respect to, the collection of intelligence – and especially signals intelligence. The United States Intelligence

* This is an edited, reformatted and augmented version of a document released by the White House, January 17, 2014.

Community (IC) has achieved remarkable success in developing enhanced capabilities to perform its signals intelligence mission in this rapidly changing world, and these enhanced capabilities are a major reason we have been able to adapt to a dynamic and challenging security environment.[1] The United States must preserve and continue to develop a robust and technologically advanced signals intelligence capability to protect our security and that of our partners and allies. Our signals intelligence capabilities must also be agile enough to enable us to focus on fleeting opportunities or emerging crises and to address not only the issues of today, but also the issues of tomorrow, which we may not be able to foresee.

Advanced technologies can increase risks, as well as opportunities, however, and we must consider these risks when deploying our signals intelligence capabilities. The IC conducts signals intelligence activities with care and precision to ensure that its collection, retention, use, and dissemination of signals intelligence account for these risks. In light of the evolving technological and geopolitical environment, we must continue to ensure that our signals intelligence policies and practices appropriately take into account our alliances and other partnerships; the leadership role that the United States plays in upholding democratic principles and universal human rights; the increased globalization of trade, investment, and information flows; our commitment to an open, interoperable and secure global Internet; and the legitimate privacy and civil liberties concerns of U.S. citizens and citizens of other nations.

Presidents have long directed the acquisition of foreign intelligence and counterintelligence[2] pursuant to their constitutional authority to conduct U.S. foreign relations and to fulfill their constitutional responsibilities as Commander in Chief and Chief Executive. They have also provided direction on the conduct of intelligence activities in furtherance of these authorities and responsibilities, as well as in execution of laws enacted by the Congress. Consistent with this historical practice, this directive articulates principles to guide why, whether, when, and how the United States conducts signals intelligence activities for authorized foreign intelligence and counterintelligence purposes.[3]

SECTION 1. PRINCIPLES GOVERNING THE COLLECTION OF SIGNALS INTELLIGENCE

Signals intelligence collection shall be authorized and conducted consistent with the following principles:

a) The collection of signals intelligence shall be authorized by statute or Executive Order, proclamation, or other Presidential directive, and undertaken in accordance with the Constitution and applicable statutes, Executive Orders, proclamations, and Presidential directives.
b) Privacy and civil liberties shall be integral considerations in the planning of U.S. signals intelligence activities. The United States shall not collect signals intelligence for the purpose of suppressing or burdening criticism or dissent, or for disadvantaging persons based on their ethnicity, race, gender, sexual orientation, or religion. Signals intelligence shall be collected exclusively where there is a foreign

intelligence or counterintelligence purpose to support national and departmental missions and not for any other purposes.

c) The collection of foreign private commercial information or trade secrets is authorized only to protect the national security of the United States or its partners and allies. It is not an authorized foreign intelligence or counterintelligence purpose to collect such information to afford a competitive advantage[4] to U.S. companies and U.S. business sectors commercially.

d) Signals intelligence activities shall be as tailored as feasible. In determining whether to collect signals intelligence, the United States shall consider the availability of other information, including from diplomatic and public sources. Such appropriate and feasible alternatives to signals intelligence should be prioritized.

SECTION 2. LIMITATIONS ON THE USE OF SIGNALS INTELLIGENCE COLLECTED IN BULK

Locating new or emerging threats and other vital national security information is difficult, as such information is often hidden within the large and complex system of modern global communications. The United States must consequently collect signals intelligence in bulk[5] in certain circumstances in order to identify these threats. Routine communications and communications of national security interest increasingly transit the same networks, however, and the collection of signals intelligence in bulk may consequently result in the collection of information about persons whose activities are not of foreign intelligence or counterintelligence value. The United States will therefore impose new limits on its use of signals intelligence collected in bulk. These limits are intended to protect the privacy and civil liberties of all persons, whatever their nationality and regardless of where they might reside.

In particular, when the United States collects nonpublicly available signals intelligence in bulk, it shall use that data only for the purposes of detecting and countering: (1) espionage and other threats and activities directed by foreign powers or their intelligence services against the United States and its interests; (2) threats to the United States and its interests from terrorism; (3) threats to the United States and its interests from the development, possession, proliferation, or use of weapons of mass destruction; (4) cybersecurity threats; (5) threats to U.S. or allied Armed Forces or other U.S or allied personnel; and (6) transnational criminal threats, including illicit finance and sanctions evasion related to the other purposes named in this section. In no event may signals intelligence collected in bulk be used for the purpose of suppressing or burdening criticism or dissent; disadvantaging persons based on their ethnicity, race, gender, sexual orientation, or religion; affording a competitive advantage to U.S. companies and U.S. business sectors commercially; or achieving any purpose other than those identified in this section.

The Assistant to the President and National Security Advisor (APNSA), in consultation with the Director of National Intelligence (DNI), shall coordinate, on at least an annual basis, a review of the permissible uses of signals intelligence collected in bulk through the National Security Council Principals and Deputies Committee system identified in PPD-1 or any successor document. At the end of this review, I will be presented with recommended additions to or removals from the list of the permissible uses of signals intelligence collected in bulk.

The DNI shall maintain a list of the permissible uses of signals intelligence collected in bulk. This list shall be updated as necessary and made publicly available to the maximum extent feasible, consistent with the national security.

SECTION 3. REFINING THE PROCESS FOR COLLECTING SIGNALS INTELLIGENCE

U.S. intelligence collection activities present the potential for national security damage if improperly disclosed. Signals intelligence collection raises special concerns, given the opportunities and risks created by the constantly evolving technological and geopolitical environment; the unique nature of such collection and the inherent concerns raised when signals intelligence can only be collected in bulk; and the risk of damage to our national security interests and our law enforcement, intelligence-sharing, and diplomatic relationships should our capabilities or activities be compromised. It is, therefore, essential that national security policymakers consider carefully the value of signals intelligence activities in light of the risks entailed in conducting these activities.

To enable this judgment, the heads of departments and agencies that participate in the policy processes for establishing signals intelligence priorities and requirements shall, on an annual basis, review any priorities or requirements identified by their departments or agencies and advise the DNI whether each should be maintained, with a copy of the advice provided to the APNSA.

Additionally, the classified Annex to this directive, which supplements the existing policy process for reviewing signals intelligence activities, affirms that determinations about whether and how to conduct signals intelligence activities must carefully evaluate the benefits to our national interests and the risks posed by those activities.[6]

SECTION 4. SAFEGUARDING PERSONAL INFORMATION COLLECTED THROUGH SIGNALS INTELLIGENCE

All persons should be treated with dignity and respect, regardless of their nationality or wherever they might reside, and all persons have legitimate privacy interests in the handling of their personal information.[7] U.S. signals intelligence activities must, therefore, include appropriate safeguards for the personal information of all individuals, regardless of the nationality of the individual to whom the information pertains or where that individual resides.[8]

a) *Policies and Procedures.* The DNI, in consultation with the Attorney General, shall ensure that all elements of the IC establish policies and procedures that apply the following principles for safeguarding personal information collected from signals intelligence activities. To the maximum extent feasible consistent with the national security, these policies and procedures are to be applied equally to the personal information of all persons, regardless of nationality:[9]

I. *Minimization.* The sharing of intelligence that contains personal information is necessary to protect our national security and advance our foreign policy interests, as it enables the United States to coordinate activities across our government. At the same time, however, by setting appropriate limits on such sharing, the United States takes legitimate privacy concerns into account and decreases the risks that personal information will be misused or mishandled. Relatedly, the significance to our national security of intelligence is not always apparent upon an initial review of information: intelligence must be retained for a sufficient period of time for the IC to understand its relevance and use it to meet our national security needs. However, long-term storage of personal information unnecessary to protect our national security is inefficient, unnecessary, and raises legitimate privacy concerns. Accordingly, IC elements shall establish policies and procedures reasonably designed to minimize the dissemination and retention of personal information collected from signals intelligence activities.
   - Dissemination: Personal information shall be disseminated only if the dissemination of comparable information concerning U.S. persons would be permitted under section 2.3 of Executive Order 12333.
   - Retention: Personal information shall be retained only if the retention of comparable information concerning U.S. persons would be permitted under section 2.3 of Executive Order 12333 and shall be subject to the same retention periods as applied to comparable information concerning U.S. persons. Information for which no such determination has been made shall not be retained for more than 5 years, unless the DNI expressly determines that continued retention is in the national security interests of the United States.

   Additionally, within 180 days of the date of this directive, the DNI, in coordination with the Attorney General, the heads of other elements of the IC, and the heads of departments and agencies containing other elements of the IC, shall prepare a report evaluating possible additional dissemination and retention safeguards for personal information collected through signals intelligence, consistent with technical capabilities and operational needs.

II. *Data Security and Access.* When our national security and foreign policy needs require us to retain certain intelligence, it is vital that the United States take appropriate steps to ensure that any personal information contained within that intelligence is secure. Accordingly, personal information shall be processed and stored under conditions that provide adequate protection and prevent access by unauthorized persons, consistent with the applicable safeguards for sensitive information contained in relevant Executive Orders, proclamations, Presidential directives, IC directives, and associated policies. Access to such personal information shall be limited to authorized personnel with a need to know the information to perform their mission, consistent with the personnel security requirements of relevant Executive Orders, IC directives, and associated policies. Such personnel will be provided appropriate and adequate training in the principles set forth in this directive. These persons may access and use the information consistent with applicable laws and Executive Orders and the principles of this directive; personal information for which no determination has been made that it can be permissibly disseminated or retained under section 4(a)(i) of this directive shall be accessed only in order to make such determinations (or to conduct authorized administrative, security, and oversight functions).

III. *Data Quality.* IC elements strive to provide national security policymakers with timely, accurate, and insightful intelligence, and inaccurate records and reporting can not only undermine our national security interests, but also can result in the collection or analysis of information relating to persons whose activities are not of foreign intelligence or counterintelligence value. Accordingly, personal information shall be included in intelligence products only as consistent with applicable IC standards for accuracy and objectivity, as set forth in relevant IC directives. Moreover, while IC elements should apply the IC Analytic Standards as a whole, particular care should be taken to apply standards relating to the quality and reliability of the information, consideration of alternative sources of information and interpretations of data, and objectivity in performing analysis.

IV. *Oversight.* The IC has long recognized that effective oversight is necessary to ensure that we are protecting our national security in a manner consistent with our interests and values.

Accordingly, the policies and procedures of IC elements, and departments and agencies containing IC elements, shall include appropriate measures to facilitate oversight over the implementation of safeguards protecting personal information, to include periodic auditing against the standards required by this section.

The policies and procedures shall also recognize and facilitate the performance of oversight by the Inspectors General of IC elements, and departments and agencies containing IC elements, and other relevant oversight entities, as appropriate and consistent with their responsibilities. When a significant compliance issue occurs involving personal information of any person, regardless of nationality, collected as a result of signals intelligence activities, the issue shall, in addition to any existing reporting requirements, be reported promptly to the DNI, who shall determine what, if any, corrective actions are necessary. If the issue involves a non-United States person, the DNI, in consultation with the Secretary of State and the head of the notifying department or agency, shall determine whether steps should be taken to notify the relevant foreign government, consistent with the protection of sources and methods and of U.S. personnel.

b) *Update and Publication.* Within 1 year of the date of this directive, IC elements shall update or issue new policies and procedures as necessary to implement section 4 of this directive, in coordination with the DNI. To enhance public understanding of, and promote public trust in, the safeguards in place to protect personal information, these updated or newly issued policies and procedures shall be publicly released to the maximum extent possible, consistent with classification requirements.

c) *Privacy and Civil Liberties Policy Official.* To help ensure that the legitimate privacy interests all people share related to the handling of their personal information are appropriately considered in light of the principles in this section, the APNSA, the Director of the Office of Management and Budget (OMB), and the Director of the Office of Science and Technology Policy (OSTP) shall identify one or more senior officials who will be responsible for working with the DNI, the Attorney General, the heads of other elements of the IC, and the heads of departments and agencies containing other elements of the IC, as appropriate, as they develop the policies and procedures called for in this section.

d) *Coordinator for International Diplomacy.* The Secretary of State shall identify a senior official within the Department of State to coordinate with the responsible departments and agencies the United States Government's diplomatic and foreign policy efforts related to international information technology issues and to serve as a point of contact for foreign governments who wish to raise concerns regarding signals intelligence activities conducted by the United States.

SECTION 5. REPORTS

a) Within 180 days of the date of this directive, the DNI shall provide a status report that updates me on the progress of the IC's implementation of section 4 of this directive.

b) The Privacy and Civil Liberties Oversight Board is encouraged to provide me with a report that assesses the implementation of any matters contained within this directive that fall within its mandate.

c) Within 120 days of the date of this directive, the President's Intelligence Advisory Board shall provide me with a report identifying options for assessing the distinction between metadata and other types of information, and for replacing the "need-to-share" or "need-to-know" models for classified information sharing with a Work-Related Access model.

d) Within 1 year of the date of this directive, the DNI, in coordination with the heads of relevant elements of the IC and OSTP, shall provide me with a report assessing the feasibility of creating software that would allow the IC more easily to conduct targeted information acquisition rather than bulk collection.

SECTION 6. GENERAL PROVISIONS

a) Nothing in this directive shall be construed to prevent me from exercising my constitutional authority, including as Commander in Chief, Chief Executive, and in the conduct of foreign affairs, as well as my statutory authority. Consistent with this principle, a recipient of this directive may at any time recommend to me, through the APNSA, a change to the policies and procedures contained in this directive.

b) Nothing in this directive shall be construed to impair or otherwise affect the authority or responsibility granted by law to a United States Government department or agency, or the head thereof, or the functions of the Director of OMB relating to budgetary, administrative, or legislative proposals. This directive is intended to supplement existing processes or procedures for reviewing foreign intelligence or counterintelligence activities and should not be read to supersede such processes and procedures unless explicitly stated.

c) This directive shall be implemented consistent with applicable U.S. law and subject to the availability of appropriations.

d) This directive is not intended to, and does not, create any right or benefit, substantive or procedural, enforceable at law or in equity by any party against the United States, its departments, agencies, or entities, its officers, employees, or agents, or any other person.

End Notes

[1] For the purposes of this directive, the terms "Intelligence Community" and "elements of the Intelligence Community" shall have the same meaning as they do in Executive Order 12333 of December 4, 1981, as amended (Executive Order 12333).

[2] For the purposes of this directive, the terms "foreign intelligence" and "counterintelligence" shall have the same meaning as they have in Executive Order 12333. Thus, "foreign intelligence" means "information relating to the capabilities, intentions, or activities of foreign governments or elements thereof, foreign organizations, foreign persons, or international terrorists," and "counterintelligence" means "information gathered and activities conducted to identify, deceive, exploit, disrupt, or protect against espionage, other intelligence activities, sabotage, or assassinations conducted for or on behalf of foreign powers, organizations, or persons, or their agents, or international terrorist organizations or activities." Executive Order 12333 further notes that "[i]ntelligence includes foreign intelligence and counterintelligence."

[3] Unless otherwise specified, this directive shall apply to signals intelligence activities conducted in order to collect communications or information about communications, except that it shall not apply to signals intelligence activities undertaken to test or develop signals intelligence capabilities.

[4] Certain economic purposes, such as identifying trade or sanctions violations or government influence or direction, shall not constitute competitive advantage.

[5] The limitations contained in this section do not apply to signals intelligence data that is temporarily acquired to facilitate targeted collection. References to signals intelligence collected in "bulk" mean the authorized collection of large quantities of signals intelligence data which, due to technical or operational considerations, is acquired without the use of discriminants (e.g., specific identifiers, selection terms, etc.).

[6] Section 3 of this directive, and the directive's classified Annex, do not apply to (1) signals intelligence activities undertaken by or for the Federal Bureau of Investigation in support of predicated investigations other than those conducted solely for purposes of acquiring foreign intelligence; or (2) signals intelligence activities undertaken in support of military operations in an area of active hostilities, covert action, or human intelligence operations.

[7] Departments and agencies shall apply the term "personal information" in a manner that is consistent for U.S. persons and non-U.S. persons. Accordingly, for the purposes of this directive, the term "personal information" shall cover the same types of information covered by "information concerning U.S. persons" under section 2.3 of Executive Order 12333.

[8] The collection, retention, and dissemination of information concerning "United States persons" is governed by multiple legal and policy requirements, such as those required by the Foreign Intelligence Surveillance Act and Executive Order 12333. For the purposes of this directive, the term "United States person" shall have the same meaning as it does in Executive Order 12333.

[9] The policies and procedures of affected elements of the IC shall also be consistent with any additional IC policies, standards, procedures, and guidance the DNI, in coordination with the Attorney General, the heads of IC elements, and the heads of any other departments containing such elements, may issue to implement these principles. This directive is not intended to alter the rules applicable to U.S. persons in Executive Order 12333, the Foreign Intelligence Surveillance Act, or other applicable law.

In: Balancing Liberty, Privacy, and Security ... ISBN: 978-1-63117-999-0
Editor: Benji Norwood

Chapter 4

FACT SHEET: THE ADMINISTRATION'S PROPOSAL FOR ENDING THE SECTION 215 BULK TELEPHONY METADATA PROGRAM*

Office of the Press Secretary

ABSTRACT

On January 17, 2014, President Obama gave a speech at the Department of Justice on his Administration's review of certain intelligence activities. During this speech, he ordered a transition that would end the Section 215 bulk telephony metadata program as it previously existed and establish a new mechanism to preserve the capabilities we need without the government holding this bulk metadata. The President made clear that he was ordering this transition to give the public greater confidence that their privacy is appropriately protected, while maintaining the tools our intelligence and law enforcement agencies need to keep us safe. This fact sheet describes the steps the Administration has taken to implement this transition, details the President's proposal for a new program to replace the Section 215 program, and outlines the steps the Administration will be taking in the near future to realize the President's vision.

ENDING THE SECTION 215 BULK TELEPHONY METADATA PROGRAM AS IT EXISTED

On January 17, 2014, the President directed the first step in the transition of the Section 215 program; that the Department of Justice (DOJ) to seek to modify the program to ensure that:

* This is an edited, reformatted and augmented version of a document released by the White House, March 27, 2014.

- Absent an emergency situation, the government can query the telephony metadata collected pursuant to the program only after a judge approves the use of specific numbers for such queries based on national security concerns; and
- The results of any query are limited to metadata within two hops of the selection term being used, instead of three.

On February 5, 2014, the Foreign Intelligence Surveillance Court (FISC) approved the government's request to modify the program.

The President's Proposal to Replace the Section 215 Program

For the second step in the transition, the President instructed the Attorney General and the Intelligence Community (IC) to develop options for a new program that could match the capabilities and fill the gaps that the Section 215 metadata program was designed to address without the government holding the bulk telephony metadata records. The President further instructed the Attorney General and the IC to report back to him with options for alternative approaches before the program comes up for reauthorization by the FISC on March 28th.

Consistent with this directive, DOJ and the IC developed options designed to meet the criteria the President laid out in his speech -- to preserve the capabilities we need without the government holding this metadata. The Administration has also consulted with Congress, the private sector, privacy and civil liberties groups, and other interested groups.

On the basis of these consultations, and after having carefully considered the available options, the President has decided on a proposal that will, with the passage of appropriate legislation, allow the government to end bulk collection of telephony metadata records under Section 215, while ensuring that the government has access to the information it needs to meet its national security requirements. Under the President's proposal, a new program would be created with the following key attributes:

- the government will not collect these telephone records in bulk; rather, the records would remain at the telephone companies for the length of time they currently do today;
- absent an emergency situation, the government would obtain the records only pursuant to individual orders from the FISC approving the use of specific numbers for such queries, if a judge agrees based on national security concerns;
- the records provided to the government in response to queries would only be within two hops of the selection term being used, and the government's handling of any records it acquires will be governed by minimization procedures approved by the FISC;
- the court-approved numbers could be used to query the data over a limited period of time without returning to the FISC for approval, and the production of records would be ongoing and prospective; and

- the companies would be compelled by court order to provide technical assistance to ensure that the records can be queried and that results are transmitted to the government in a usable format and in a timely manner.

The President believes that this approach will best ensure that we have the information we need to meet our intelligence requirements while enhancing public confidence in the manner in which this information is collected and held.

THE PATH FORWARD

Legislation will be needed to implement the President's proposal. The Administration has been in consultation with congressional leadership and members of the Intelligence and Judiciary Committees on this important issue throughout the last year, and we look forward to continuing to work with Congress to pass a bill that achieves the goals the President has put forward. Given that this legislation will not be in place by March 28 and given the importance of maintaining the capabilities in question, the President has directed DOJ to seek from the FISC a 90-day reauthorization of the existing program, which includes the substantial modifications in effect since February.

INDEX

#

A

B

C

D

E

I

J

L

M

Q

R

S

T

U

V

W